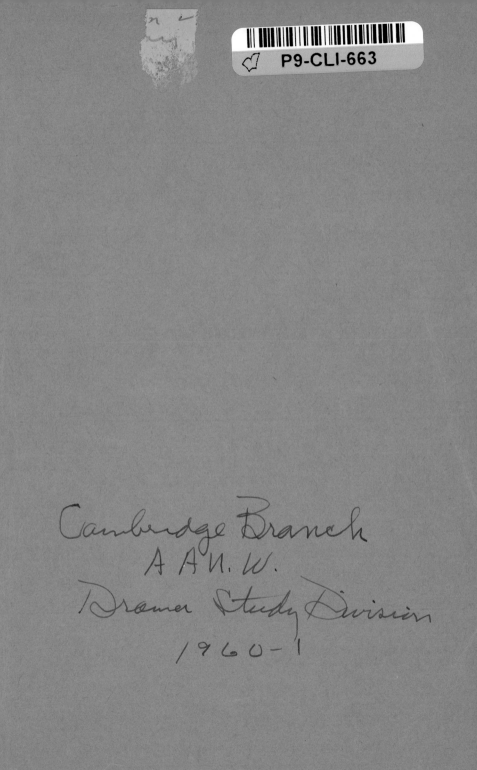

Cambridge Branch
A A U. W.
Drama Study Division
1960-1

THE TENTH MAN

Random House, New York

A new play by Paddy Chayefsky

THE TENTH MAN

To
Tyrone Guthrie

THE TENTH MAN *was first presented by Saint Subber and Arthur Cantor at The Booth Theatre, New York City, November 5, 1959, with the following cast:*

(In order of appearance)

THE CABALIST *Hirschman*	Arnold Marlé
THE SEXTON · *Bleyer*	David Vardi
SCHLISSEL	Lou Jacobi
ZITORSKY	Jack Gilford
ALPER	George Voskovec
FOREMAN	Jacob Ben-Ami
THE GIRL (EVELYN FOREMAN)	Risa Schwartz
ARTHUR LANDAU *p 34*	Donald Harron
HARRIS	Martin Garner
THE RABBI	Gene Saks
KESSLER BOYS	{ Alan Manson { Paul Marin
THE POLICEMAN	Tim Callaghan

Directed by Tyrone Guthrie
Settings and lighting by David Hays
Costumes by Frank Thompson
Associate: Caroline Swann

An Orthodox Synagogue

ACT ONE

Before the Morning Prayers.

ACT TWO

Scene 1: The Morning Prayers.
Scene 2: Before the Afternoon Prayers.

ACT THREE

The Exorcism.

ACT ONE

ACT ONE

Interior of the synagogue of the Congregation Atereth-Tifereth Yisroel.

It is a poor congregation, and the synagogue is actually a converted shop. A raised platform surrounded by a railing contains the lectern and the Holy Ark. This altar is surrounded by rows of plain wooden folding chairs which constitute the seating accommodations for the congregation. On the far side of the altar is an old desk at which THE RABBI *presides when teaching Hebrew school.*

A partitioned area downstage right is THE RABBI'S *study, a crowded little cubicle containing a battered mahogany desk and chair, an old leather armchair, a worn leather couch, and piles of black prayer books. On the walls are old framed pictures of bearded patriarchs in desolate obsession over their Talmuds and perhaps a few familiar scenes from the Old Testament.*

Downstage is a metal heating unit. There is a second heating unit upstage, and a door leading apparently to a bathroom. The front door is stage left.

It is 6:30 A.M. on a cold winter day.

At rise, THE CABALIST *stands in the middle of the synagogue, entirely wrapped in a thick white linen prayer shawl with broad black stripes, praying silently from a heavy prayer book that rests on the railing of the altar. Suddenly he pauses in his intense de-*

3

votions, clutches at the railing as if to keep himself from falling. We have the impression that he is faint, near to swooning. He is a small, bearded man, in his seventies; his face is lean and lined, his eyes sunken and hollow. He wears a small black skullcap from beneath which stick out gray forelocks and sidecurls—a testament to his orthodoxy. After a moment, he regains his strength and returns to his prayers.

Three men hurry into the synagogue out of the oppressive cold of the street. They are THE SEXTON, SCHLISSEL *and* ZITORSKY. *They all wear heavy overcoats and gray fedoras.* SCHLISSEL *and* ZITORSKY *are in their early seventies.* THE SEXTON *is a small, nervous, bespectacled man of forty-eight. We know he is a sexton because he carries a huge ring of keys. The men rub their hands for warmth and huff and puff and dart quick looks at* THE CABALIST, *who is oblivious to their entrance.*

SCHLISSEL

(*Muttering*)

Close the door. (*Light pours down on the synagogue as* THE SEXTON *flicks on the wall switch.* THE SEXTON *scurries upstage to fuss with the heater in the rear of the synagogue.* SCHLISSEL and ZITORSKY *shuffle downstage to a small uncovered heater and stand silently—indeed a little wearily—for a moment.* SCHLISSEL *sighs*) So how goes it with a Jew today?

ZITORSKY

How should it go?

SCHLISSEL

Have a pinch of snuff.

ZITORSKY

No, thank you.

4

SCHLISSEL

Davis won't be here this morning. I stopped by his house. He
has a cold. His daughter-in-law told me he's still in bed.

ZITORSKY

My daughter-in-law, may she grow rich and buy a hotel with a
thousand rooms and be found dead in every one of them.

SCHLISSEL

My daughter-in-law, may she invest heavily in General Mo-
tors, and the whole thing should go bankrupt.

ZITORSKY

Sure, go have children.

SCHLISSEL

The devil take them all.

THE SEXTON

(*Scurrying downstage; to* THE CABALIST *as he passes*)
Hirschman, are you all right?
(*He flutters, a small round ball of a man, to the door of* THE
RABBI'S *office, which he now opens with one of the many
keys on his chain.*)

SCHLISSEL

Foreman won't be here today.

ZITORSKY

What's the matter with Foreman?

SCHLISSEL

His granddaughter today. This is the morning.

ZITORSKY

Oh, that's right. Today is the morning.

SCHLISSEL

Listen, it's better for everybody.

ZITORSKY

Sure.

SCHLISSEL

I told Foreman, I said: "Foreman, it's better for everybody." The girl is becoming violent. I spoke to her father. He said to me they live in terror what she'll do to the other children. They came home one night, they found her punching one of the little children.

ZITORSKY

Well, what can you do?

SCHLISSEL

What can you do? You do what they're doing. They're putting her back in the institution.

ZITORSKY

Of course. There she will have the benefit of trained psychiatric personnel.

SCHLISSEL

The girl is incurable. She's been in and out of mental institutions since she was eleven years old. I met the psychiatrist there, you know, when I was up there to visit Foreman last week. I discussed the whole business with him. A fine young fellow. The girl is a schizophrenic with violent tendencies.

(ZITORSKY *considers this diagnosis for a moment, then sighs.*)

ZITORSKY

Ah, may my daughter-in-law eat acorns and may branches sprout from her ears.

SCHLISSEL

May my daughter-in-law live to be a hundred and twenty, and may she have to live all her years in *her* daughter-in-law's house.

(THE SEXTON *has been tugging a large opened brown cardboard carton out of* THE RABBI's *office, from which he now extracts two velvet bags which he hands to* SCHLISSEL *and* ZITORSKY. *A fifth old Jew now enters from the street, a patrician little man with a Vandyke beard and a black homburg. His name is* ALPER. *He bursts into shrill prayer as he enters.*)

ALPER

(*Chanting*)

"As for me in the abundance of thy loving kindness will I come into thy house; I will worship toward thy holy temple in the fear of thee. How goodly are thy tents, O Jacob . . ." (*As precipitously as the prayer had begun, it now drops into nothing more than a rapid movement of lips.* THE SEXTON *acknowledges* ALPER's *arrival with a nod and darts back into* THE RABBI's *office, where he plunks himself behind the desk and begins hurriedly to dial the phone.* ALPER's *voice zooms abruptly up into a shrill incantation again*) ". . . in the truth of thy salvation. Amen!"

SCHLISSEL

Amen.

7

ZITORSKY

Amen.

(ALPER *joins the other two old men and they stand in silent, rueful speculation.*)

THE SEXTON

(*On phone*)

Hello, Harris? This is Bleyer the Sexton. Come on down today, we need you. Foreman won't be here. Davis is sick. We won't have ten men for the morning prayers if you don't come down . . . Services start in twenty minutes. Hurry up . . . Wear a sweater under your coat . . . All right . . .

(*He hangs up, takes a large ledger from the desk, and begins nervously to examine its pages.*)

SCHLISSEL

Hirschman slept over in the synagogue again last night. Have you ever seen such pietistic humbug?

ALPER

Well, he is a very devout man. A student of the cabala. The Rabbi speaks of him with the greatest reverence.

SCHLISSEL

Devout indeed. I assure you this lavish display of orthodoxy is a very profitable business. I was told confidentially just yesterday that his board and food are paid for by two foolish old women who consider him a saint.

ALPER

It can't cost them very much. He's been fasting the last three days.

8

SCHLISSEL

And the reason he sleeps in the synagogue so frequently is because his landlady does not give him heat for his own room in the mornings.

ZITORSKY

Ah, go be an old man in the winter.

ALPER

I must say, I really don't know what to do with myself on these cold days.

SCHLISSEL

I'm an atheist. If I had something better to do, would I be here?

ZITORSKY

You know what would be a nice way to kill a day? I think it would be nice to take a trip up to Mount Hope Cemetery and have a look at my burial plot. A lovely cemetery. Like a golf course, actually. By the time one gets there and comes back, the whole day has been used up. Would you like to come? I'll pay both your fares.

ALPER

Why not? I have never been to Mount Hope. I have my burial plot on Mount Zion Cemetery.

ZITORSKY

Oh, that's a beautiful cemetery.

ALPER

Yes, it is. My wife wanted to buy plots in Cedar Lawn because her whole family is buried there, but I wouldn't hear of it.

9

ZITORSKY

Oh, Cedar Lawn. I wouldn't be buried in Cedar Lawn.

ALPER

It's in such a bad state. The headstones tumble one on top of the other, and everybody walks on the graves.

ZITORSKY

They don't take care in Cedar Lawn. My wife once said, she should rest in peace, that Cedar Lawn was the tenement of cemeteries.

ALPER

A well-turned phrase.

ZITORSKY

She had a way with words, God grant her eternal rest.

ALPER

I'd like you to come to Mount Zion sometimes, see my plot.

ZITORSKY

Maybe we could make the trip tomorrow.

SCHLISSEL

Listen to these two idiots, discussing their graves as if they were country estates.

ZITORSKY

Where are you buried, Schlissel?

SCHLISSEL

Cedar Lawn.

ALPER

Well, listen, there are many lovely areas in Cedar Lawn. All my wife's family are buried there.

ZITORSKY

Come with us, Schlissel, and have a look at my grave.

SCHLISSEL

Why not? What else have I got to do?

(ALPER *now slowly goes about the business of donning his prayer shawl and phylacteries, which he takes out of a velvet prayer bag. Among Jews, prayer is a highly individual matter, and peripatetic to the bargain. The actual ritual of laying on the phylacteries is a colorful one.* ALPER *extracts his left arm from his jacket and rebuttons his jacket so that his shirt-sleeved left arm hangs loose. Then, the shirt sleeve is rolled up almost to the shoulder, and the arm phylactery, a long thin black leather thong, is put on by wrapping it around the left arm seven times, three times around the palm, and three times around the middle finger. All this is accompanied by rapidly recited prayers, as is the laying on of the head phylactery. All the while* ALPER *walks, bending and twisting at the knees, raising his voice occasionally in the truly lovely words of incantation. In a far upstage corner,* THE CABALIST *huddles under his enveloping white tallith—prayer shawl—his back to everyone else, deeply involved in his personal meditations. The synagogue itself is a shabby little place, the walls yellowed and cracked, illumined by a fitful overhead bulb. There is indeed at this moment a sense of agelessness, even of primitive barbarism. During this,* THE SEXTON *has dialed a second number.*)

THE SEXTON

Hello? Mr. Arnold Kessler, please . . . How do you do? This is Mr. Bleyer the Sexton at the synagogue. Perhaps you recall me . . . Did I wake you up? I'm terribly sorry. As long as you're up, according to my books, your father died one year ago yesterday, on the eleventh day in the month of Shvat, may his soul fly straight to the Heavenly Gates, and how about coming down with your brother and saying a memorial prayer in your father's name? . . . Let me put it this way, Mr. Kessler. You know we can't have morning prayers without a quorum of ten men. If you and your brother don't come down we won't have a quorum . . . As a favor to me . . . Kessler, may your children be such devoted sons, and bring your brother. You are doing a good deed. Peace be with you. Hurry up.

> (*He hangs up, sits frowning, totaling up on his fingers the number of men he has, scowls. In the synagogue,* ALPER's *voice rises for a brief moment.*)

ALPER

". . . and it shall be to thee for a sign upon thy hand, and for a memorial between thy eyes . . ."

> (THE SEXTON *rises abruptly from his chair and bustles out of the office to the front door of the synagogue.*)

THE SEXTON

(*To nobody in particular*)

Listen, I'm going to have to get a tenth Jew off the street somewheres. I'll be right back. Schlissel, will you please fix that bench already, you promised me.

> (*He exits.* SCHLISSEL *nods and picks up a hammer. For a moment, only the singsong murmur of the rapid prayers and the upstage tapping of* SCHLISSEL's *hammer fill the*

*stage. The front door to the synagogue now opens, and a
sixth old Jew peers in. He is a frightened little wisp of a
man, named* FOREMAN. *He is obviously in a state. He darts
terrified looks all about the synagogue, and then abruptly
disappears back into the street, leaving the synagogue
door open. Nobody noticed his brief appearance. A moment later, he is back, this time leading a slim young girl
of eighteen wearing a topcoat, who is also distracted. The
old man herds her quickly across the synagogue to* THE
RABBI'S *office, pushes her in, and closes the door behind
her. She stands in* THE RABBI'S *office, almost rigid with
terror.* FOREMAN *scuttles back to close the front door.*
SCHLISSEL *looks up and notices* FOREMAN *and nods to him;
he nods back. Like his friends,* FOREMAN *wears a heavy
winter coat and a worn fedora some sizes too small for
him. He stands and watches the others apprehensively.
At last* ALPER *reaches the end of his laying on of the
phylacteries, his voice climbing to a shrill incantation.*)

ALPER

(*To* FOREMAN, *moving slowly as he prays*)

". . . and it shall be for a sign upon thy hand, and for frontlets
between thy eyes; for by strength of hand the Lord brought us
out from Egypt. Amen!"

FOREMAN

(*Muttering, his head bobbing nervously*)

Amen!

ALPER

I thought you weren't coming down today, Foreman.

FOREMAN

(*His mouth working without saying anything. Finally, he says*)
Alper . . .

ALPER

You seem agitated. Is something wrong?

FOREMAN

(*Staring at his friend*)
Alper, I have her here.

ALPER

You have who here?

FOREMAN

I have my granddaughter Evelyn here. I have her here in the
Rabbi's office.

ALPER

What are you talking about?

FOREMAN

I took her out of the house while nobody was looking, and I
brought her here. I am faint. Let me sit down.
(*He sinks onto a chair. His friend regards him with concern.*)

ALPER

Here, David, let me take your coat.

FOREMAN

Alper, I have seen such a thing and heard words as will place
me in my grave before the singing of the evening service.

"Blessed art Thou, O Lord, King of the Universe, who hath wrought the wonders of the world." (*Suddenly half-starting from his seat*) I must speak to Hirschman! This is an affair for Hirschman who has delved into the cabala and the forbidden mysteries of numbers.

ALPER

Sit down, Foreman, and compose yourself. (FOREMAN *sinks slowly back onto his chair*) Why did you bring her here? Foreman, you are my oldest friend from our days in the seminary together in Rumni in the Province of Poltava, and I speak to you harshly as only a friend may speak. You are making too much out of this whole matter of the girl. I know how dear she is to you, but the girl is insane, for heaven's sakes! What sort of foolishness is this then to smuggle her out of your son's home? To what purpose? Really, Foreman, a gentle and pious man like you! Your son must be running through the streets at this moment shouting his daughter's name. Call him on the phone and tell him you are bringing her back to him.

(FOREMAN *stares at his friend, his pale eyes filled with tears.*)

FOREMAN

Alper . . .

ALPER

David, my dear friend, make peace with this situation.

FOREMAN
(*Whispering*)

She is possessed, Alper. She has a dybbuk in her. A demon! It spoke to me. (*He stares down at the floor at his feet, a numb terror settling over his face*) It spoke to me. I went into my granddaughter this morning to comfort her, and I said: "How are you?" And she seemed quite normal. She has these moments of absolute lucidity. (*He looks desperately at his friend again*) She seemed to know she was being taken to the institution again. Then suddenly she fell to the floor in a swoon. I said: "Evelyn, what's the matter?" And she looked up at me, and it was no longer her face, but a face so twisted with rage that my blood froze in my body. And a voice came out of her that was not her own. "Do you know my voice?" And I knew it. I knew the voice. God have mercy on my soul. I stood there like a statue, and my granddaughter lay on the floor with her eyes closed, and the voice came out of her, but her lips never moved. "David Foreman, son of Abram, this is the soul of Hannah Luchinsky, whom you dishonored and weakened in your youth, and the Gates of Heaven are closed to me." And my granddaughter began to writhe on the floor as if in the most horrible agony, and she began to laugh so loudly that I was sure my son and daughter-in-law in the living room could hear. I flung the door open in panic, and my son and daughter-in-law were sitting there talking, and they heard nothing. And I tell you shrieks of laughter were coming from this girl on the floor. And I closed the door and besought God, and finally the dybbuk was silent. May God strike me down on this spot, Alper, if every word I tell you is not true.

(ALPER *has slowly sat down on an adjacent chair, absolutely enthralled by the story. He stares at* FOREMAN.)

ALPER

A dybbuk?

FOREMAN
(*Nodding*)
A dybbuk. Could you believe such a thing?

ALPER

Who did the dybbuk say she was?

FOREMAN

You should remember her. Hannah Luchinsky.

ALPER

The name is vaguely familiar.

FOREMAN

You remember Luchinsky, the sexton of the Rumni seminary,
with his three daughters? Hannah was the handsome one who
became pregnant, and they threw stones at her, called her harlot,
and drove her out of the city.

ALPER

(*Recognition slowly coming over him*)

Ooohhh.

FOREMAN

I was the one who debased her.

ALPER

You? You were such a nose-in-the-books, a gentle and modest
fellow. Dear me. A dybbuk. Really! What an extraordinary
thing. Schlissel, do you want to hear a story?

SCHLISSEL

(*Coming over*)

What?

ALPER

(*To* ZITORSKY, *who ambles over*)

Listen to this. Foreman is telling a story here that will turn
your blood into water.

17

SCHLISSEL

What happened?

FOREMAN

What happened, Schlissel, was that I went in to see my granddaughter this morning and discovered that she was possessed by
a dybbuk. Now, please, Schlissel, before you go into one of your
interminable disputations on the role of superstition in the capitalist economy, let me remind you that I am a follower of Mai-
monides and . . .

SCHLISSEL

What are you talking about?

FOREMAN

A dybbuk! A dybbuk! I tell you my granddaughter is possessed by a dybbuk! Oh, my head is just pounding! I do not
know which way to turn.

SCHLISSEL

What are you prattling about dybbuks?

ALPER

(*To* SCHLISSEL)

The voice of Hannah Luchinsky spoke to him through the lips
of his granddaughter.

ZITORSKY

Oh, a dybbuk.

SCHLISSEL

What nonsense is this?

ALPER

(*To* FOREMAN)

Are you sure?

FOREMAN

(*Angrily*)

Am I sure? Am I a peasant who leaps at every black cat? Have I ever shown a susceptibility to mysticism? Have you not seen me engaging Hirschman over there in violent disputation over the fanatic numerology of the cabala? Have I not mocked to his very face the murky fantasy of the Gilgul with wispy souls floating in space? Really! Am I sure! Do you take me for a fool, a prattler of old wives' tales? Really! I tell you I heard that woman's voice as I hear the cold wind outside our doors now, and saw my granddaughter writhing in the toils of possession as I see the phylactery on your brow this moment. I was a teacher of biology for thirty-nine years at the Yeshiva High School. A dedicated follower of the great Rambam who scoffed at augurs and sorcerers! For heaven's sakes! Really! I report to you only what I see! (*He strides angrily away, and then his brief flurry of temper subsides as abruptly as it flared*) My dear Alper, please forgive this burst of temper. I am so distressed by this whole business that I cannot control my wits. I assure you that it is as hard for me to believe my own senses as it is for you.

ZITORSKY

When I was a boy in Lithuania, there was a young boy who worked for the butcher who was possessed by the dybbuk.

SCHLISSEL

(*Scornfully*)

A dybbuk. Sure. Sure. When I was a boy in Poland, I also heard stories about a man who lived in the next town who was possessed by a dybbuk. I was eight years old, and, one day after school, my friends and I walked barefoot the six miles to the next town, and we asked everybody, "Where is the man with the dybbuk?" And nobody knew what we were talking about. So I came home and told my mother: "Mama, there is no man with a dybbuk in the next town." And she gave me such a slap across the face that I turned around three times. And she said to me: "Aha! Only eight years old and already an atheist." Foreman, my friend, you talk like my mother, who was an ignorant fishwife. I am shocked at you.

FOREMAN

Oh, leave me be, Schlissel. I have no patience with your pontificating this morning.

ALPER

Don't let him upset you, Foreman. The man is a Communist.

FOREMAN

He is not a Communist. He is just disagreeable.

SCHLISSEL

My dear fellow, I have never believed in God. Should I now believe in demons? A dybbuk. This I would like to see.

FOREMAN

(Furiously)

Then see! (He strides to the door of THE RABBI's office and wrenches the door open. The others gingerly follow him to the opened doorway and peer in. THE GIRL—EVELYN—stares at them, terrified. In a thunderous voice, FOREMAN cries out—) Dybbuk! I direct you to reveal yourself!

(THE GIRL stares at the four patently startled old men, and

then suddenly bursts into a bloodcurdling shriek of laughter. The four old men involuntarily take one step back and regard this exhibition wide-eyed.)

FOREMAN

What is your name?

THE GIRL

I am Hannah Luchinsky.

FOREMAN

Who are you?

THE GIRL

I am the Whore of Kiev, the companion of sailors.

FOREMAN

How come you to be in my granddaughter's body?

THE GIRL

I was on a yacht in the sea of Odessa, the pleasure of five wealthy merchants. And a storm arose, and all were lost. And my soul rose from the water and flew to the city of Belgorod where my soul appealed to the sages of that city. But since I was debauched they turned their backs on me.

FOREMAN

And then?

THE GIRL

Then my soul entered the body of a cow who became insane and was brought to slaughter and I flew into the body of this girl as if divinely directed.

FOREMAN

What do you want?

THE GIRL

I want the strength of a pure soul so that I may acquire that experience to ascend to heaven.

FOREMAN

I plead with you to leave the body of this girl.

THE GIRL

I have wandered through Gilgul many years, and I want peace. Why do you plague me? There are those among you who have done the same as I and will suffer a similar fate. There is one among you who has lain with whores many times, and his wife died of the knowledge.

ZITORSKY

(*Aghast*)

Oh, my God!

THE GIRL

(*Laughing*)

Am I to answer questions of old men who have nothing to do but visit each other's cemeteries?

ZITORSKY

(*Terrified*)

A dybbuk . . . a dybbuk . . .

FOREMAN

Evelyn . . . Evelyn . . . She is again in a catatonic state.

(THE GIRL *now sits in* THE RABBI's *chair, sprawling wan-*

22

tonly, apparently finished with the interview. The four old men regard her a little numbly. They are all quite pale as a result of the experience. After a moment, FOREMAN *closes the door of* THE RABBI'S *office, and the four old men shuffle in a silent group downstage, where they stand, each reviewing in his own mind the bizarre implications of what they have seen.* FOREMAN *sinks into a chair and covers his face with his hands. After a long, long moment,* ZITORSKY *speaks.)*

ZITORSKY

Well, that's some dybbuk, all right.

SCHLISSEL

The girl is as mad as a hatter and fancies herself a Ukrainian trollop. This is a dybbuk?

ALPER

I found it quite an unnerving experience.

ZITORSKY

She caught me dead to rights. I'll tell you that. I was the one she was talking about there, who trumpeted around with women. Listen, when I was in the garment business, if you didn't have women for the out-of-town buyers, you couldn't sell a dozen dresses. Oh, I was quite a gamy fellow when I was in business, a madcap really. One day, my wife caught me in the shop with a model—who knew she would be downtown that day?—and from that moment on, my wife was a sick woman and died three years later, cursing my name with her last breath. That was some dybbuk, all right. How she picked me out! It gave me the shivers.

23

ALPER

Did you notice her use of archaic language and her Russian accent? The whole business had an authentic ring to me.

SCHLISSEL

What nonsense! The last time I was up to Foreman's the girl confided to me in a whisper that she was Susan Hayward. A dybbuk! Ever since she was a child Foreman has been pumping her head full of the wretched superstitions of the Russian Pale, so she thinks she is a dybbuk. The girl is a lunatic and should be packed off to an asylum immediately.

(ALPER *regards* SCHLISSEL *with a disapproving eye; he then takes* SCHLISSEL's *arm and leads him a few steps away for a private chat.*)

ALPER

Really, Schlissel, must you always be so argumentative? We are all here agreed that we have a dybbuk in our company, but you always seem intent on being at odds with everyone around you. Really, look at poor Foreman, how distraught he is. Out of simple courtesy, really, for an old friend, can you not affect at least a silence on the matter? And, after all, what else have you got to do today? Ride two and a half hours to look at Zitorsky's tombstone? When you stop and think of it, this dybbuk is quite an exciting affair. Really, nothing like this has happened since Kornblum and Milsky had that fist fight over who would have the seat by the East Wall during the High Holidays.

ZITORSKY

(*Ambling over*)

That's some dybbuk, all right.

SCHLISSEL

(*Frowning*)

All right, so what'll we do with this dybbuk now that we got it?

ALPER

It seems to me, there is some kind of ritual, an exorcism of sorts.

ZITORSKY

Maybe we should tell the Rabbi.

SCHLISSEL

A young fellow like that. What does he know of dybbuks? A dybbuk must be exorcised from the body by a rabbi of some standing. You can't just call in some smooth-shaven young fellow fresh from the seminary for such a formidable matter as a dybbuk. This Rabbi has only been here two months. He hardly knows our names.

ALPER

He's right. You have to get a big rabbi for such a business.

SCHLISSEL

What has to be done is we must get in touch with the Korpotchniker Rabbi of Williamsburg, who has inherited the mantle of the Great Korpotchniker of Lwów, whose fame extends to all the corners of the world.

ZITORSKY

Oh, a sage among sages.

ALPER

I was about to suggest the Bobolovitcher Rabbi of Crown Heights.

SCHLISSEL

Where do you come to compare the Bobolovitcher Rabbi with the Korpotchniker?

ALPER

I once attended an afternoon service conducted by the Bobolovitcher, and it was an exalting experience. A man truly in the great tradition of Chassidic rabbis.

ZITORSKY

A sage among sages, may his name be blessed for ever and ever.

SCHLISSEL

It shows how much you know. The Bobolovitcher Rabbi is a disciple of the Korpotchniker and sat at the Korpotchniker's feet until a matter of only a few years ago.

ALPER

Listen, I'm not going to argue with you. Either one is fine for me.

SCHLISSEL

The Korpotchniker is the number one Chassidic rabbi in the world. If you're going to involve yourself at all, why not go straight to the top?

ALPER

All right, so let it be the Korpotchniker.

ZITORSKY

For that matter, the Lubanower Rabbi of Brownsville is a man of great repute.

SCHLISSEL

The Lubanower! Really! He's a young man, for heaven's sakes!

ALPER

Zitorsky, let it be decided then that it will be the Korpotchniker.

ZITORSKY

I only made a suggestion.

SCHLISSEL

The question is how does one get to the Korpotchniker? One does not drop into his home as if it were a public library. One has to solicit his secretary and petition for an audience. It may take weeks.

ALPER

I do think, Schlissel, we shall have to get a more accessible rabbi than that. Ah, here is Hirschman, who I am sure can give us excellent counsel in this matter.

(THE CABALIST *has indeed finished his prayers, and is shuffling downstage, a small, frightened man.* FOREMAN *leaps from his chair.*)

FOREMAN

Hirschman!

(*Everyone crowds around* THE CABALIST.)

ZITORSKY

Oh, boy, Hirschman, have we got something to tell you!

ALPER

Zitorsky, please. Hirschman, you are a man versed in the cabala, a man who prays with all the seventy-two names of the Most Ancient of the Ancient Ones.

FOREMAN

(*Blurting out*)

Hirschman, my granddaughter is possessed by a dybbuk!

THE CABALIST

(*Starting back in terror*)

A dybbuk!

ALPER

Foreman, please, one does not announce such a thing as baldly as that.

THE CABALIST

Are you sure?

FOREMAN

Hirschman, as a rule, I am not given to whimsy.

THE CABALIST

Was it the soul of a woman wronged in her youth?

FOREMAN

Yes.

THE CABALIST

I heard her cry out last night. I awoke for my midnight devotions, and as I prayed I heard the whimpering of a woman's soul.

(*A strange expression of wonder settles over his face*) I have fasted three days and three nights, and I dismissed the sound of this dybbuk as a fantasy of my weakened state. For only those to whom the Ancient One has raised his veil can hear the traffic of dybbuks. Is this a sign from God that my penitence is over? I have prayed for such a sign. I have felt strange things these past days. Sudden, bursting illuminations have bleached mine eyes, and I have heard the sounds of dead and supernatural things.

> (*He lifts his worn little face, his eyes wide with wonder. The others are put a little ill-at-ease by this effusive outburst.* FOREMAN, *indeed, is quite overwhelmed.*)

ALPER

Actually, Hirschman, all we want to know is if you knew the telephone number of the Korpotchniker Rabbi.

> (THE CABALIST *with some effort brings himself back to the moment at hand.*)

THE CABALIST

He is my cousin. I will call him for you.

> (*He moves slowly off, still obsessed with some private wonder of his own, to the phone on the outside wall of* THE RABBI's *office.*)

ALPER

(*Quite awed*)

Your cousin? You are the Korpotchniker's cousin, Hirschman?

ZITORSKY

(*Hurrying after* THE CABALIST)

You'll need a dime, Hirschman.

> (*He gives* THE CABALIST *the ten-cent piece.*)

29

ALPER

Schlissel, the Korpotchniker's cousin, did you hear? Apparently, he's not such a humbug.

SCHLISSEL

I tell you, he gives me the creeps, that Hirschman.
(THE CABALIST *has dialed a number on the wall phone.*
FOREMAN *stands at his elbow, hunched with anxiety.*)

THE CABALIST

(*To* FOREMAN, *gently*)
Where is she, the dybbuk?

FOREMAN

In the Rabbi's office.

THE CABALIST

You are wise to go to the Korpotchniker. He is a Righteous One among the Righteous Ones. We were quite close as children until I abandoned the rabbinate. (*On the phone, in soft, gentle tones*) Hello? Is this Chaim son of Yosif . . . This is Israel son of Isaac . . . And peace be unto you . . . There is a man here of my congregation who feels his granddaughter is possessed by a dybbuk and would seek counsel from my cousin . . . He will bless you for your courtesy. Peace be unto you, Chaim son of Yosif. (*He hangs the receiver back in its cradle and turns to* FOREMAN) Give me a paper and pencil. (*The others, who have crowded around to hear the phone call, all seek in their pockets for a paper and pencil and manage to produce an old envelope and a stub of a pencil between them*) That was the Korpotchniker's secretary, and you are to go to his home as quickly as you can. I will write the address down for you. It is in Williamsburg in Brooklyn. And you will be received directly after the morning services.

(He gives FOREMAN *the address, sweeps his prayer shawl on and retires upstage again for continued devotions.)*

FOREMAN

Thank you, Hirschman. The eye of the Lord will be open to you in the time of your need.

ZITORSKY

Oh, Williamsburg. That's quite a ride from here.

SCHLISSEL

What are you talking about? Foreman, you take the Long Island Railroad to Atlantic Avenue Station, where you go downstairs, and you catch the Brooklyn subway.

ALPER

Maybe, I should go along with you, David, because a simple fellow like you will certainly get lost in the Atlantic Avenue Station, which is an immense conflux of subways.

SCHLISSEL

What you do, Foreman, is you take the Long Island Railroad to the Atlantic Avenue Station, where you take the Double G train on the lower level . . .

ALPER

Not the Double G train.

SCHLISSEL

What's wrong with the Double G?

31

ALPER

One takes the Brighton train. The Double G train will take him to Smith Street, which is a good eight blocks' walk.

SCHLISSEL

The Brighton train will take him to Coney Island.

ALPER

Foreman, listen to what I tell you. I will write down the instructions for you because an innocent fellow like you, if they didn't point you in the right direction, you couldn't even find the synagogue in the morning. Where's my pencil?
(*He has taken the paper and pencil from* FOREMAN's *numb fingers and is writing down the traveling instructions.*)

FOREMAN

(*Staring off at the wall of* THE RABBI's *office*)
What shall I do with the girl? I can't leave her here.

ALPER

Don't worry about the girl. She knows me. I'm like a second grandfather to her.

FOREMAN

I don't like to leave her. Did I do right, Alper? Did I do right, kidnaping her this morning and bringing her here? Because the psychiatrist said we must prepare ourselves that she would probably spend the rest of her life in mental institutions. The irrevocability of it! The rest of her life! I was in tears almost the whole night thinking about it. Perhaps this produced a desperate susceptibility in me so that I clutch even at dybbuks rather than believe she is irretrievably insane. Now, in the sober chill of afterthought, it all seems so unreal and impetuous. And here I am

bucketing off to some forbidding rabbi to listen to mystical incantations.

ALPER

The Korpotchniker is not a rogue, Foreman. He is not going
to sell you patent medicine. He will advise you quite sensibly, I
am sure.

FOREMAN

(*Buttoning his coat*)
Yes, yes, I shall go to see him. You shall have to hide her till I
come back. My son has probably called the police by now, and
sooner or later they will come here looking for her.

ALPER

Don't worry about it. I won't leave her side for a moment.

FOREMAN

I better tell her I'm going. She'll be frightened if she looks for
me, and I'm not here.
(*He hurries quickly to* THE RABBI's *office, where he stands
a moment, regarding* THE GIRL *with mingled fear and ten-
derness.* THE GIRL *has sunk into the blank detachment of
schizophrenia and stares unseeingly at the floor.*)

SCHLISSEL

So the girl is a fugitive from the police. The situation is beginning to take on charm.

ALPER

Look at Schlissel. The retired revolutionary. As long as it's
against the law, he believes in dybbuks.

SCHLISSEL

I believe in anything that involves a conspiracy.
(*At this point, the front door bursts open, and* THE SEXTON
returns with the announcement—)

THE SEXTON

I've got a tenth Jew!

ZITORSKY

Sexton, have we got something to tell you!

SCHLISSEL

(*Shushing him abruptly*)
Sha! Idiot! Must you tell everyone?

THE SEXTON

(*He leans back through the open door to the street and says
to someone out there*)
Come in, come in . . . (*A fine-looking, if troubled, young fellow in his middle thirties enters; he is dressed in expensive
clothes, albeit a little shabby at the moment, as if he had been on
a bender for the last couple of days. His name is* ARTHUR LANDAU.
*He stands ill-at-ease and scowling, disturbed in aspect. His bur-
berry topcoat hangs limply on him.* THE SEXTON *has scooted to an
open carton, from which he takes out a black paper skullcap,
nervously talking as he does*) Harris didn't come in yet?

SCHLISSEL

No.

THE SEXTON

The two Kessler boys, I called them on the phone, they didn't
show up yet? (*He thrusts the skullcap into* ARTHUR's *hand*)
Here's a skullcap, put it on. (ARTHUR *takes the skullcap absently,*

but makes no move to put it on. He is preoccupied with deep and dark thoughts. THE SEXTON *heads for the front door*) The Rabbi's not here yet?

SCHLISSEL

He'll be here in a couple of minutes.

THE SEXTON

It's only seven minutes to the services. Listen, I'm going to the Kesslers'. I'll have to pull them out of their beds, I can see that. I'll be right back. (*To* ARTHUR) You'll find some phylacteries in the carton there. Alper, give the man a prayer book. Sure, go find ten Jews on a winter morning.
(*He exits, closing the front door.*)

FOREMAN

(*As he comes out of the office*)
All right, I'm going. She didn't eat anything this morning, so see she gets some coffee at least. Let's see. I take the Long Island Railroad to Atlantic Avenue Station. Listen, it has been a number of years since I have been on the subways. Well, wish me luck. Have I got money for carfare? Yes, yes. Well . . . well . . . my dear friends, peace be with you.

ALPER

And with you, Foreman.

ZITORSKY

Amen.

FOREMAN

(*Opening the door*)
Oh, it's cold out there.
(*He exits, closing the door.*)

ALPER

He'll get lost. I'm sure of it.

ZITORSKY

Oh, have you ever seen such excitement? My heart is fairly pounding.

ALPER

Oh, it's just starting. Now comes the exorcism. That should be something to see.

ZITORSKY

Oh, boy.

SCHLISSEL

Oh, I don't know. You've seen one exorcism, you've seen them all.

ZITORSKY

You saw one, Schlissel?

SCHLISSEL

Sure. When I was a boy in Poland, we had more dybbuks than we had pennies. We had a fellow there in my village, a mule driver, a burly chap who reeked from dung and was drunk from morning till night. One day, he lost his wits completely, and it was immediately attributed to a dybbuk. I was a boy of ten, perhaps eleven, and I watched the whole proceedings through a hole in the roof of the synagogue. A miracle-working rabbi who was passing through our district was invited to exorcise the dybbuk. He drew several circles on the ground and stood in the center surrounded by four elders of the community, all dressed in white linen and trembling with terror. The Miracle-Worker bellowed out a series of incantations, and the poor mule driver, who was beside himself with fear, screamed and . . . hello, Harris . . . (*This last is addressed to a very, very old man named* HARRIS, *who is making his halting way into the synagogue at this moment. He barely nods to the others, having all he can do to get into the synagogue and close the door.* SCHLISSEL *continues his blithe story*) . . . and fell to the floor. It was a marvelous vaudeville, really. I was so petrified that I fell off the roof and almost broke a leg. The Miracle-Worker wandered off to work other miracles and the mule driver sold his mule and went to America where I assume, because he was a habitual drunkard and an insensitive boor, he achieved considerable success. Our little village had a brief month of notoriety, and we were all quite proud of ourselves.

ALPER

Oh, it sounds like a marvelous ceremony.

SCHLISSEL

Of course, they don't exorcise dybbuks like they used to. Nowadays, the rabbi hangs a small amulet around your neck, intones, "Blessed art Thou, O Lord," and that's an exorcism.

ALPER

Oh, I hope not.

SCHLISSEL

Really, religion has become so pallid recently, it is hardly worth while being an atheist.

ZITORSKY

I don't even know if I'll come to see this exorcism. I'm already shivering just hearing about it.

ALPER

Well, you know, we are dealing with the occult here, and it is quite frightening. Hello there, Harris, how are you? (*By now, the octogenarian has removed his overcoat, under which he wears several layers of sweaters, one of which turns out to be one of his grandson's football jerseys, a striped red garment with the number 63 on it. For the rest of the act, he goes about the business of putting on his phylacteries.* ALPER *claps his hands*) Well, let me find out if we can help this young Jew here. (*He moves toward* ARTHUR LANDAU, *smiling*) Can I give you a set of phylacteries?

ARTHUR

(*Scowling—a man who has had a very bad night the night before*)
I'm afraid I wouldn't have the first idea what to do with them.

ALPER

You'll find a prayer shawl in one of these velvet bags here.

ARTHUR

No, thank you.

ALPER

(*Offering a small black prayer book*)
Well, here's a prayer book anyway.

ARTHUR

Look, the only reason I'm here is a little man stopped me on the street, asked me if I was Jewish, and gave me the impression he would kill himself if I didn't come in and complete your quorum. I was told all I had to do was stand around for a few minutes wearing a hat. I can't read Hebrew and I have nothing I want to pray about, so there's no sense giving me that book. All I want to know is how long is this going to take, because I don't feel very well, and I have a number of things to do.

ALPER

My dear young fellow, you'll be out of here in fifteen or twenty minutes.

ARTHUR

Thank you.
(*He absently puts the black paper skullcap on his head and sits down, scowling, on one of the wooden chairs.* ALPER *regards him for a moment; then turns and goes back to his two colleagues.*)

ALPER

(*To* SCHLISSEL *and* ZITORSKY)
To such a state has modern Jewry fallen. He doesn't know what phylacteries are. He doesn't want a shawl. He can't read Hebrew.

ZITORSKY

I wonder if he's still circumcised.
(ARTHUR *abruptly stands.*)

ARTHUR

I'd like to make a telephone call. (*Nobody hears him. He repeats louder*) I said, I'd like to make a telephone call.

39

ALPER

(*Indicating the wall phone*)
Right on the wall there.

ARTHUR

This is a rather personal call.

ALPER

There's a phone in the Rabbi's office there.
(ARTHUR *crosses to* THE RABBI's *office.*)

SCHLISSEL

Well, look about you, really. Here you have the decline of Orthodox Judaism graphically before your eyes. This is a synagogue? A converted grocery store, flanked on one side by a dry cleaner and on the other by a shoemaker. Really, if it wasn't for the Holy Ark there, this place would look like the local headquarters of the American Labor Party. In Poland, where we were all one step from starvation, we had a synagogue whose shadow had more dignity than this place.

ALPER

It's a shame and a disgrace.

ZITORSKY

A shame and a disgrace.
(*In* THE RABBI's *office* ARTHUR *is regarding* THE GIRL *with a sour eye.*)

ARTHUR

Excuse me. I'd like to make a rather personal call.
(THE GIRL *stares down at the floor, unhearing, unmoving,*

off in a phantasmic world of her own distorted creation.
ARTHUR *sits down at* THE RABBI'S *desk, turns his shoulder*
to THE GIRL, *and begins to dial a number.*)

SCHLISSEL

Where are all the Orthodox Jews? They have apostated to the
Reform Jewish temples, where they sit around like Episcopa-
lians, listening to organ music.

ALPER

Your use of the word "apostasy" in referring to Reform Jews
interests me, Schlissel. Is it not written in Sifre on Deuteronomy,
"Even if they are foolish, even if they transgress, even if they are
full of blemishes, they are still called sons"? So, after all, is it so
terrible to be a Reform Jew? Is this not an interesting issue for
disputation? Oh, my God!

(*He wheels and starts back for* THE RABBI'S *office. The*
same thought has been entering the other two old fellows'
minds, as has been indicated by a growing frown of con-
sternation on each of their faces. They follow ALPER *to* THE
RABBI'S *office, where he opens the door quickly and stares*
in at ARTHUR LANDAU. *The latter is still seated at* THE
RABBI'S *desk, waiting for an answer to his phone call; and*
THE GIRL *is still in her immobilized state.* ARTHUR *casts*
such a baleful eye at this interruption that the three old
men back out of the office and close the door. They re-
main nervously outside the door of the office. At last,
someone responds to ARTHUR'S *phone call.*)

ARTHUR

(*On the phone, shading his face, and keeping his voice down*)
Hello, Doctor, did I wake you up? This is Arthur Landau

. . . Yes, I know. Do you think you can find an hour for me this morning? . . . Oh, I could be in your office in about an hour or so. I'm out in Mineola. My ex-wife lives out here with her parents, you know. And I've been blind drunk for—I just figured it out—three days now. And I just found myself out here at two o'clock in the morning banging on their front door, screaming . . . (THE GIRL'S *presence bothers him. He leans across the desk to her and says*—) Look, this is a very personal call, and I would really appreciate your letting me have the use of this office for just a few minutes.

(THE GIRL *looks up at him blankly.*)

THE GIRL

(*Hollowly*)

I am the Whore of Kiev, the companion of sailors.

(*The bizarreness of this stops* ARTHUR. *He considers it for a moment, and then goes back to the phone.*)

ARTHUR

(*On the phone*)

No, I'm still here. I'm all right. At least, I'm still alive. (*He hides his face in the palm of one hand and rubs his brow nervously*) I've got to see you, Doc. Don't hang up on me, please. If my analyst hangs up on me, that'll be the end. Just let me talk a couple of minutes . . . I'm in some damned synagogue. I was on my way to the subway. Oh, my God, I've got to call my office. I was supposed to be in court twice yesterday. I hope somebody had the brains to apply for an adjournment. So it's funny, you know. I'm in this damned synagogue. I'll be down in about an hour, Doctor . . . Okay. Okay . . . I'm all right . . . No, I'm all right . . . I'll see you in about an hour. (*He hangs up, hides his face in the palms of both hands and slowly pulls himself together. After a moment, he looks up at* THE GIRL, *who is back to staring at the floor. He frowns, stands, goes to the door of the office, opens it, gives one last look at* THE GIRL, *and closes the door behind him. He finds himself staring at the inquiring faces of the three old men*) Listen, I hope you know there's a pretty strange girl in there.

(*The old men bob their heads nervously.* ARTHUR *crosses the synagogue to a chair and sits down, his face dark with his emotions. The three old men regard him anxiously. After a moment,* SCHLISSEL *approaches* ARTHUR.)

SCHLISSEL

A strange girl, you say?

ARTHUR

Yes.

SCHLISSEL

Did she say anything?

ARTHUR

She said: "I am the Whore of Kiev, the companion of sailors."

SCHLISSEL

That was a very piquant statement, wouldn't you say?

ARTHUR

Yes, I think I would call it piquant.

SCHLISSEL

What do you make of it?

43

ARTHUR

(*Irritably*)

Look, I'm going. I have a hundred things to do. I . . .

SCHLISSEL

No, no, no. Sit down. For heaven's sakes, sit down.

ALPER

(*Hurrying over*)

Don't go. Oh, my, don't go. We need you for a tenth man. We haven't had ten men in the morning in more than a week, I think.

ZITORSKY

(*On* ALPER's *tail*)

Two weeks, at least.

(*At this point,* HARRIS, *who has finally divested himself of his muffler and the heavy, ribbed sweaters which were over his jacket, and is now enwrapt in a prayer shawl, bursts into a high, quavering prayer.*)

HARRIS

"Blessed art thou, O Lord, our God, King of the Universe, who hath sanctified us by his commandments and . . ."

(*The words dribble off into inaudibility.* ARTHUR LANDAU *darts a startled look at the old man, not being prepared for this method of prayer, and moves a few nervous steps away from the other old men, then stands rubbing his brow, quite agitated.*)

44

ALPER

(*Whispering to* SCHLISSEL)
So what happened in there? Did she say anything?

SCHLISSEL

Yes, she said she was the Whore of Kiev, and the companion of sailors.

ALPER

Oh, dear me.

SCHLISSEL

I'm afraid we shall have to get her out of the Rabbi's office because if she keeps telling everybody who walks in there that she is the Whore of Kiev, they will pack us all off to the insane asylum. And let us be quite sensible about this situation. If Foreman has kidnaped the girl, he has kidnaped her, however kindly his motives—not that I expect the police to regard a dybbuk as any kind of sensible explanation. Whatever the case, it would be a good idea to keep the girl a little less accessible. (*The wall phone rings*) Ah! I'll tell you who that is. That's Foreman's son calling to find out if Foreman and the girl are here. (*The phone rings again*) Well, if you won't answer it, I'll answer it.
(*He crosses to the wall phone.*)

ALPER

We could take her to my house. Everybody is still sleeping. We'll put her in the cellar.
(*The phone rings again.* SCHLISSEL *picks up the phone.*)

45

SCHLISSEL

(*On the phone*)

Hello. (*He turns to the others and nods his head, indicating he was quite right in guessing the caller. The other two old men move closer to the phone*) Mr. Foreman, your father isn't here . . . Listen, I tell you, he isn't here . . . I wouldn't have the slightest idea. I haven't seen her since I was up to your house last Tuesday. Isn't she home? . . . If he comes in, I'll tell him . . . Okay . . . (*He hangs up and turns to the other two*) Well, we are in it up to our necks now.

ALPER

(*Stripping off his phylacteries*)

So shall we take her to my house?

SCHLISSEL

All right. Zitorsky, go in and tell her we are going to take her some place else.

ZITORSKY

(*Not exactly inspired by the idea*)

Yeah, sure.

SCHLISSEL

(*To ZITORSKY*)

For heaven's sakes, Zitorsky, you don't really believe that's a dybbuk in there.

ZITORSKY

If that's no dybbuk, then you go in and take her.

(SCHLISSEL *shuffles slowly to the door of* THE RABBI'S *office.*)

46

SCHLISSEL

(*Pausing at the closed office door*)
It's getting kind of complicated. Maybe we ought to call Foreman's son and tell him she's here and not get involved.

ZITORSKY

Oh, no!

SCHLISSEL

Ah, well, come on. What can they do to us? They'll call us foolish old men, but then foolishness is the only privilege of old age. So, Alper, you'll deal with her. You know how to talk to her, and we'll hide her in your cellar. So we'll have a little excitement. (*He opens the door, and the three old men regard* THE GIRL *as she sits in sodden, detached immobility*) Listen. Alper, let's get along, you know. Before the Sexton comes back and starts asking us where we're all going.
(ALPER *nods apprehensively and takes a few steps into the office.*)

ALPER

(*To* THE GIRL, *who doesn't actually hear him or know of his presence*)
How do you do, my dear Evelyn. This is Alper here. (*She makes no answer.* ALPER *turns to the other two*) She's in one of her apathetic states.

ZITORSKY

(*Darting back into the synagogue proper*)
I'll get your coat, Alper.

47

SCHLISSEL

(*Looking around to see if* ARTHUR *is paying any attention to what's going on; he is not*)
Well, take her by the arm.

ALPER

Evelyn, your grandfather suggested we take you to my house. You always liked to play with the children's toys in my cellar there, you remember? Come along, and we'll have a good time.

ZITORSKY

(*Giving* SCHLISSEL *an overcoat*)
Here. Give this to Alper.
(*He hurries off to the front door of the synagogue.*)

HARRIS

(*In the process of laying on his phylacteries*)
"And from thy wisdom, O Most High God, Thou shalt reserve for me . . ."
(*He dribbles off into inaudibility.*)

ALPER

(*Placing a tentative hand on* THE GIRL'S *shoulder*)
Evelyn, dear . . .
(*She looks up, startled.*)

ZITORSKY

(*Leaning out the front door, searching up and down the street*)
Oh, it's cold out here.

48

ALPER

(*To* SCHLISSEL, *who is hurriedly putting on his own overcoat*)
I have a feeling we're going to have trouble here.

SCHLISSEL

I've got your coat here.

ALPER

Evelyn . . . (*A strange animal-like grunt escapes* THE GIRL, *and she begins to moan softly*) Evelyn dear, please don't be alarmed. This is Mr. Alper here who has known you since you were born. (*He is getting a little panicky at the strange sounds coming out of* THE GIRL, *and he tries to grab her arm to help her to her feet. She bursts into a shrill scream, electrifying everybody in the synagogue with the exception of* THE CABALIST, *who is oblivious to everything.* ZITORSKY, *who has just closed the front door, stands frozen with horror.* ARTHUR, *sunk in despondency, looks up, startled. The old man,* HARRIS, *pauses briefly, as if the sound has been some distant buzzing, and then goes back to his mumbled prayers*) Evelyn, my dear girl, for heaven's sakes . . .

THE GIRL

(*Screaming out*)
Leave me alone! Leave me alone!

ARTHUR

(*Coming to* SCHLISSEL, *who shuts the office door quickly*)
What's going on in there?

SCHLISSEL

It's nothing, it's nothing.

THE GIRL
(*Screaming*)
They are my seven sons! My seven sons!

ALPER
(*Who is trying earnestly to get out of the office*)
Who closed this door?

ZITORSKY
(*Reaching for the front door*)
I'm getting out of here.

SCHLISSEL
(*To* ZITORSKY)
Where are you going?
(*But* ZITORSKY *has already fled into the street.*)

ARTHUR
(*To* SCHLISSEL)
What's all this screaming?
(ALPER, *at last out of the office, comes scurrying to* SCHLISSEL.)

ALPER
I put my hand on her arm to help her up, and she burst into this fit of screaming.
(ARTHUR *strides to the open doorway of the office.* THE GIRL *stares at him, hunched now in terror, frightened and at bay.*)

50

ARTHUR

(*To* SCHLISSEL)

What have you been doing to this girl?

SCHLISSEL

The girl is possessed by a dybbuk.

ARTHUR

What?

SCHLISSEL

(*To* ALPER)

Zitorsky ran out in the street like a kangaroo.

ALPER

Listen, maybe we should call somebody.

ARTHUR

Listen, what is this?

ALPER

My dear young man, there is no reason to alarm yourself. There is an insane girl in the Rabbi's office, but she appears to have quieted down.

ARTHUR

What do you mean, there's an insane girl in the Rabbi's office?

ALPER

Yes, she is a catatonic schizophrenic, occasionally violent, but really, go back to your seat. There is no cause for alarm.

51

ARTHUR

Am I to understand, sir, that it is a practice of yours to keep insane girls in your Rabbi's office?

ALPER

No, no. Oh, dear, I suppose we shall have to tell him. But you must promise, my dear fellow, to keep this whole matter between us. (*To* SCHLISSEL) Zitorsky, you say, took to his heels?

SCHLISSEL

Absolutely flew out of the door.

ALPER

Well, I really can't blame him. It was quite an apprehensive moment. I was a little shaken myself. (*He peeks into the office*) Yes, she seems to be quite apathetic again. I think we just better leave her alone for the time being.

ARTHUR

Look, what is going on here?

ALPER

My dear fellow, you are, of course, understandably confused. The girl, you see, is possessed by a dybbuk.

ARTHUR

Yes, of course. Well, that explains everything.

ALPER

Well, of course, how would he know what a dybbuk is? A dybbuk is a migratory soul that possesses the body of another human being in order to return to heaven. It is a Lurian doctrine, actually tracing back to the Essenes, I suppose, but popularized during the thirteenth century by the Spanish cabalists. I wrote several articles on the matter for Yiddish periodicals. My name is Moyshe Alper, and at one time I was a journalist of some repute. (ZITORSKY *appears in the doorway again, peering nervously in*) Come in, Zitorsky, come in. The girl is quiet again. (ZITORSKY *approaches them warily*.)

ARTHUR

Look, are you trying to tell me you have a girl in there you think is possessed by some demon? Where is her mother or father or somebody who should be responsible for her?

ALPER

If there were someone responsible for her, would she be insane in the first place?

ARTHUR

Of course, this is none of my business . . .

ALPER

You are a good fellow and let me put you at ease. The girl is in good hands. Nobody is going to hurt her. Her grandfather, who adores her more than his own life, has gone off for a short while.

ZITORSKY

To Williamsburg on the Brighton train.

SCHLISSEL

The Brighton train takes you to Coney Island.

53

ZITORSKY

You said the Double G.

ALPER

All right, all right.

ARTHUR

Of course, this is none of my business.

ALPER

(*To* ARTHUR)

I can understand your concern; it shows you are a good fellow, but really the matter is well in hand.

(*The front door opens and there now enter* THE SEXTON *and two young men in their thirties, apparently the* KESSLER *boys, who are none too happy about being roused on this cold winter morning. They stand disconsolately around in the back of the synagogue.*)

THE SEXTON

Here are two more, the Kessler boys.

ALPER

Now we'll have ten for a quorum.

ZITORSKY

Kessler? Kessler? Oh, yes, the stationery store. I knew your father.

(*There is a general flurry of movement.* THE SEXTON *hurries about the ritual of baring his left arm, donning the prayer shawl and phylacteries, walking nervously about,*) *mumbling his prayers rapidly.* ARTHUR, *quite disturbed again, looks into* THE RABBI's *office at* THE GIRL, *then moves slowly into the office.* THE GIRL *is again in a world of her own. He closes the door and studies* THE GIRL. SCHLISSEL, ALPER *and* ZITORSKY *watch him warily, taking off their overcoats again and preparing to stay for the impending services.* HARRIS' *shrill quavering voice suddenly leaps up into audibility again.*)

HARRIS

"Thou shalt set apart all that openeth the womb of the Lord, and the firstling that cometh of a beast which thou shalt have, it shall belong to the Lord . . ."

SCHLISSEL

(*To* ALPER)

What are we going to do when the Rabbi tries to get into his office? He'll see the girl, and that will be the end of our exorcism. What shall we tell the Rabbi?

(*The front door of the synagogue opens, and* THE RABBI *comes striding efficiently in, right on cue. He is a young man in his early thirties, neatly dressed if a little threadbare, and carrying a briefcase.*)

ZITORSKY

Peace be with you, Rabbi.

THE RABBI

Peace be with you.

ALPER

(*Intercepting* THE RABBI *as he heads for his office*)
How do you do, Rabbi.

(THE RABBI *nods as he strides to the door of his office, where* SCHLISSEL *blocks the way.*)

SCHLISSEL

We have ten men today, Rabbi.

THE RABBI

Good. (*He reaches for the door to his office*) I'll just get my phylacteries.

ALPER

(*Seizing* ZITORSKY's *phylacteries*)
Oh, here, use these. It's late, Rabbi.

THE RABBI

(*Taking the phylacteries*)
Fine. Well, let's start the services.
(*He turns back to the synagogue proper. From all around, each man's voice rises into prayer.*)

The Curtain Falls

ACT TWO

SCENE I

Fifteen minutes later.
ZITORSKY *is reading the prayers. He stands before the lectern on the raised platform, singing the primitive chants.*

ZITORSKY

"And we beseech thee according to thine abundant mercies, O Lord . . ."

THE SEXTON

Young Kessler, come here and open the Ark.
    (*The younger* KESSLER *ascends the platform and opens the Ark by drawing the curtains and sliding the doors apart.*)

ZITORSKY

"And it came to pass, when the ark set forward, that Moses said, Rise up, O Lord, and Thine enemies shall be scattered, and they that hate Thee shall flee before Thee. For out of Zion shall go forth the Law, and the word of the Lord from Jerusalem." (*Immediately, the rest of the quorum plunges into a mumbled response: "Blessed be Thy name, O Sovereign of the World!*

59

*Blessed be Thy crown, and Thy abiding place!" Jewish prayers
are conducted in a reader-congregation pattern, although frequently the reader's vocalized statements and the congregation's
mumbled responses merge and run along simultaneously. In this
specific moment of prayer, when the Ark has been opened and
the Torah is about to be taken out, the demarcation between
reader and congregation is clear-cut. The sliding brown wooden
doors of the Ark are now open.* THE SEXTON *is reaching in to take
out the exquisitely ornamented Torah, which, when its lovely
brocaded velvet cover is taken off, will show itself to be a large
parchment scroll divided on two carved rollers. When* THE SEX-
TON *gets the Torah out, he hands it carefully to* ZITORSKY, *who has
been chosen this day for the honor of holding the Torah until it
is to be read from.* ZITORSKY, *who, as today's reader, has been reading along with the congregation although more audibly, now al-
lows his voice to ring out clearly, marking the end of this paragraph of prayers)* ". . . May it be Thy gracious will to open my
heart in Thy Law, and to grant my heart's desires, and those of
all Thy people Israel, for our benefit, throughout a peaceful life."
(Pause) "Magnify the Lord with me, and let us exalt His name
together." *(Again, the congregation leaps into mumbled response.* "Thine, O Lord, is the greatness, and the power, and the
glory, and the victory, and the majesty . . ." ZITORSKY *marches
solemnly to the front of the lectern, carrying the Torah before
him. Each man kisses the Torah as it passes him. There is now
the ritual of removing the velvet cover, and the Torah is laid
upon the lectern.* ZITORSKY, HARRIS *and* THE SEXTON *form a hover-
ing group of three old betallithed Jews over it.* THE RABBI *stands
rocking slightly back and forth to the left of the lectern. Off the
raised platform, but immediately by the railing, stands* THE CABA-
LIST, *rocking back and forth and praying.* ALPER *and* SCHLISSEL

stand at various places, mumbling their responses. The two KESS-
LER *boys have removed their coats and wear prayer shawls, but
still stand as close to the front door as they can.* ARTHUR LANDAU
stands, leaning against the wall of THE RABBI's *office, quite in-
trigued by the solemn prayers and rituals.* THE GIRL *is still in* THE
RABBI's *office, but she is standing now, listening as well as she can
to the prayers. Her face is peaceful now and quite lovely. Again*
ZITORSKY's *voice rises to indicate the end of a paragraph of
prayer)* "Ascribe all of your greatness unto our God, and render
honor to the Law."

> (*There is now a quick mumbled conference among the
> three old Jews at the lectern, then* THE SEXTON *suddenly
> leans out and calls to the two* KESSLER *boys in the rear.*)

THE SEXTON

Kessler, you want to read from the Torah?

THE ELDER KESSLER

No, no, no. Get somebody else.

THE SEXTON

Alper? (ALPER *nods and makes his way to the lectern.* THE SEX-
TON's *voice, a high, whining incantation, rises piercingly into the
air, announcing the fact that Moyshe son of Abram will read
from the Torah*) Rise up, Reb Moses Ha'Kohan, son of Abram,
and speak the blessing on the Torah. "Blessed be He, who in His
Holiness gave the Law unto his people Israel, the Law of the
Lord is perfect."

CONGREGATION
(*Scattered response*)
"And ye that cleave unto the Lord your God are alive every
one of you this day."

61

ALPER

(*Now at the lectern, raises his head and recites quickly*)
"Blessed is the Lord who is to be blessed for ever and ever."

CONGREGATION

"Blessed is the Lord who is to be blessed for ever and ever."

ALPER

"Blessed art Thou, O Lord our God, King of the Universe, who hast chosen us from all peoples and hast given us Thy Law. Blessed art Thou, O Lord, who givest the Law."

CONGREGATION

Amen!

THE SEXTON

"And Moses said . . ."
> (*There are now four mumbling old Jews huddled over the lectern. It all becomes very indistinguishable;* THE SEXTON'S *piercing tenor rises audibly now and then to indicate he is reading.* ALPER *moves into the reader's position and begins to read from the Torah, bending his knees and twisting his body and hunching over the Torah, peering at the meticulous Hebrew lettering inscribed therein.* SCHLISSEL *and the* KESSLER *boys find seats where they were standing, as does* THE CABALIST. THE RABBI *and* HARRIS *are seated on the raised platform. In* THE RABBI'S *office,* THE GIRL *decides to go out into the synagogue proper. She opens the door and moves a few steps out.* ARTHUR *hears her and turns to her warily.*)

THE GIRL

(*Quite lucidly and amiably*)
Excuse me, sir, are they reading from the Torah now?

62

(She peers over ARTHUR's *shoulder toward the old men at the lectern.)*

ARTHUR

Yes, I think so.
(He watches her carefully. She seems all right now. Still, there is something excessively ingenuous about her, a tentative, wide-eyed, gently smiling innocence.)

THE GIRL

Is my grandfather here?
(She peers nervously around the synagogue.)

ARTHUR

Which one would be your grandfather?

THE GIRL

(Growing panic)
No, he's not here. I see Mr. Alper, but I don't see my grandfather.

ARTHUR

I'm sure he will be back soon.
(His calmness reassures her.)

THE GIRL

(She studies this strange young man)
I think all synagogues should be shabby because I think of God as being very poor as a child. What do you think of God as?

ARTHUR

I'm afraid I think of God as the Director of Internal Revenue.
(THE GIRL laughs brightly and then immediately smothers her laughter, aware she is in a solemn synagogue.)

63

THE GIRL

You're irreverent. (*Frowning, she goes into* THE RABBI's *office, plops down on his swivel chair, and swivels back and forth, very much like a child.* ARTHUR *follows her tentatively, studying her cautiously, yet taken by her ingenuousness. She darts a quick frightened look at him*) Were you in here just before?

ARTHUR

Well, yes.

THE GIRL

Did I—did I say anything?

ARTHUR

(*Amiably*)

Well, yes.

THE GIRL

(*Sighing*)

I see. Well, I might as well tell you. I've been to several mental institutions. (*She looks quickly at him. He smiles at her*) You don't seem very disconcerted by that.

ARTHUR

Oh, I expect it might be hard to find somebody who couldn't do with occasional confinement in a mental institution.

(*In the synagogue,* THE SEXTON *now calls* HARRIS *to read from the Torah.*)

THE GIRL

(*She frowns*)

Did my grandfather say when he would be back or where he was going?

(*She starts from her seat frightened again.*)

64

ARTHUR

I understand he'll be back soon.

THE GIRL

Are you the doctor?

ARTHUR

No. You don't have to be the least bit afraid of me.

THE GIRL

(*She brightens*)

My grandfather and I are very close. I'm much closer to him than I am to my own father. I'd rather not talk about my father, if you don't mind. It's a danger spot for me. You know, when I was nine years old, I shaved all the hair off my head because that is the practice of really Orthodox Jewish women. I mean, if you want to be a rabbi's wife, you must shear your hair and wear a wig. That's one of my compulsive dreams. I keep dreaming of myself as the wife of a handsome young rabbi with a fine beard down to his waist and a very stern face and prematurely gray forelocks on his brow. I have discovered through many unsuccessful years of psychiatric treatment that religion has a profound sexual connotation for me. Oh, dear, I'm afraid I'm being tiresome again about my psychiatric history. Really, being insane is like being fat. You can talk about nothing else. Please forgive me. I am sure I am boring you to death.

ARTHUR

No, not at all. It's nice to hear somebody talk with passion about anything, even their insanity.

THE GIRL

(*Staring at him*)

The word doesn't bother you?

ARTHUR

What word?

THE GIRL

Insanity.

ARTHUR

Good heavens, no. I'm a lawyer. Insanity in one form or another is what fills my anteroom. Besides, I'm being psychoanalyzed myself and I'm something of a bore about that too. You are a bright young thing. How old are you?

THE GIRL

Eighteen.

ARTHUR

(*Staring at her*)

My God, you're a pretty kid! I can hardly believe you are psychopathic. Are you very advanced?

THE GIRL

Pretty bad. I'm being institutionalized again. Dr. Molineaux's Sanitarium in Long Island. I'm a little paranoid and hallucinate a great deal and have very little sense of reality, except for brief interludes like this, and I might slip off any minute in the middle of a sentence into some incoherency. If that should happen, you must be very realistic with me. Harsh reality is the most efficacious way to deal with schizophrenics.

ARTHUR

You seem well read on the matter.

THE GIRL

I'm a voracious reader. I have so little else to do with myself.
Will you come and visit me at Dr. Molineaux's hospital? I am
awfully fond of you.

ARTHUR

Yes, of course, I will.

THE GIRL

It won't be as depressing an experience as you might think. If I
am not in the violent ward, I will probably be allowed to go to
the commissary and have an ice-cream soda with you. The worst
of an insane asylum is really how poorly dressed the inmates are.
They all wear old cable-stitched sweaters. I do like to look pretty.
(*A vacuous look is beginning to come across her face*) They ask
me to be in a lot of movies, you know, when I have time. Did you
see *David and Bathsheba* with Susan Hayward? That was really
me. I don't tell anybody that. They don't want me to make
movies. My mother, I mean. She doesn't even go to synagogue on
Saturday. You're the new Rabbi, you know. Sometimes, I'm the
Rabbi, but they're all afraid of me. The temple is sixty cubits long
and made of cypress and overlaid with gold. The burnished
Roman legions clank outside the gates, you know. Did you see
The Ten Commandments? I saw that Tuesday, Wednesday. I
was in that. I was the girl who danced. I was in that. Mr. Hirschman is here, too, you know, and my grandfather. Everybody's
here. Do you see that boy over there? Go away. Leave us alone
He's insane. He's really Mr. Hirschman the Cabalist. He's making a golem. You ought to come here, Rabbi.

ARTHUR

(*Who has been listening fascinated, now says firmly*)
I am not the Rabbi, Evelyn.
(*She regards him briefly.*)

THE GIRL

Well, we're making a golem and . . .

ARTHUR

You are not making a golem, Evelyn.
(*She pauses, staring down at the floor. A grimace of pain moves quickly across her face and then leaves it. After a moment, she mumbles—*)

THE GIRL

Thank you. (*Suddenly she begins to cry and she throws herself on* ARTHUR'S *breast, clinging to him, and he holds her gently, caressing her as he would a child*) Oh, I can't bear being insane.

ARTHUR

(*Gently*)
I always thought that since the insane made their own world it was more pleasurable than this one that is made for us.

THE GIRL

(*Moving away*)
Oh, no, it is unbearably painful. It is the most indescribable desolation. You are all alone in deserted streets. You cannot possibly imagine it.

ARTHUR

I'm afraid I can. I have tried to commit suicide so many times now it has become something of a family joke. Once, before I was

68

divorced, my wife stopped in to tell a neighbor before she went out to shop: "Oh, by the way, if you smell gas, don't worry about it. It's only Arthur killing himself again." Suicides, you know, kill themselves a thousand times, but one day I'll slash my wrists and I will forget to make a last-minute telephone call and there will be no stomach-pumping Samaritans to run up the stairs and smash my bedroom door down and rush me off to Bellevue. I'll make it some day—I assure you of that.

THE GIRL

(*Regarding him with sweet interest*)
You don't look as sad as all that.

ARTHUR

Oh, I have made a profession of ironic detachment. It depresses me to hear that insanity is as forlorn as anything else. I had always hoped to go crazy myself some day since I have apparently no talent for suicide.

THE GIRL

I always thought life would be wonderful if I were only sane.

ARTHUR

Life is merely dreary if you're sane, and unbearable if you are sensitive. I cannot think of a more meaningless sham than my own life. My parents were very poor so I spent the first twenty years of my life condemning the rich for my childhood nightmares. Oh, I was quite a Bernard Barricade when I was in college. I left the Communist Party when I discovered there were easier ways to seduce girls. I turned from reproaching society for my loneliness to reproaching my mother, and stormed out of her house to take a room for myself on the East Side. Then I fell in

69

love—that is to say, I found living alone so unbearable I was willing to marry. She married me because all her friends were marrying somebody. Needless to say, we told each other how deeply in love we were. We wanted very much to be happy. Americans, you know, are frantic about being happy. The American nirvana is a man and his wife watching television amiably and then turning off the lights and effortlessly making the most ardent love to each other. Television unfortunately is a bore and ardent love is an immense drain on one's energy. I began to work day and night at my law office, and besides becoming very successful, I managed to avoid my wife entirely. For this deceit, I was called ambitious and was respected by everyone including my wife, who was quite as bored with me as I was with her. We decided to have children because we couldn't possibly believe we were that miserable together. All this while I drove myself mercilessly for fear that if I paused for just one moment, the whole slim, trembling sanity of my life would come crashing down about my feet without the slightest sound. I went to a psychoanalyst who wanted to know about my childhood when I could barely remember whether I took a taxi or a bus to his office that day. I began to drink myself into stupors, pursuing other men's wives, and generally behaving badly. One morning, I stared into the mirror and could barely make out my features. Life is utterly meaningless. I have had everything a man can get out of life—prestige, power, money, women, children, and a handsome home only three blocks from the Scarsdale Country Club, and all I can think of is I want to get out of this as fast as I can. (*He has become quite upset by now, and has to avert his face to hide a sudden welling of tears. He takes a moment to get a good grip on himself, readopts his sardonic air and says—*) As you see, I have quite a theatrical way when I want to.

THE GIRL

(*Brightly*)

Oh, I think you are wonderfully wise.

ARTHUR

Oh, it was said best by your very own King Solomon, the wisest man who ever lived, when he wrote Ecclesiastes.

THE GIRL

Oh, King Solomon didn't write Ecclesiastes. That was written by an anonymous Jewish scholar in Alexandria. I wouldn't put too much stock in it. Weariness was all the rage among the Hellenized Jews.

ARTHUR

(*Staring at her*)

You are an amazing kid.

(*She smiles back at him exuberantly, unabashedly showing her fondness for him. It embarrasses him, and he turns away. He opens the door, and looks out into the synagogue, where the reading of the Torah has come to an end.*)

THE RABBI

(*Singing out*)

"Blessed art Thou, O Lord our God, King of the Universe, who hast given us the Law of truth, and hast planted everywhere life in our midst. Blessed art Thou, O Lord, who givest the Law."

(*There is a scattered mumbled response from the old men in the synagogue.* ZITORSKY *now takes the Torah and holds it up above his head and chants.*)

ZITORSKY

"And this is the Law which Moses set before the children of

71

Israel, according to the commandment of the Lord by the hand of Moses." (*The four men on the platform form a small group as* ZITORSKY *marches slowly back to the Ark carrying the Torah. A mumble of prayers rustles through the synagogue.* ZITORSKY'S *voice rises out*) "Let them praise the name of the Lord; for His name alone is exalted."

> (*He carefully places the Torah back into the Ark. A rumble of prayer runs through the synagogue. All the men in the synagogue are standing now.*)

ARTHUR

(*Turning to* THE GIRL)
They're putting the Torah back. Is the service over?

THE GIRL

No. I have a wonderful book I want to give to you. Mr. Hirschman, our Community Cabalist, gave it to me. It is called the Book of Splendor, a terribly mystical book. And you are a mystic, you know.

ARTHUR

Oh, am I?

THE GIRL

Yes. I never met anyone who wanted to know the meaning of life as desperately as you do. I have to get the book for you.
> (SCHLISSEL *pokes his head into the office and indicates to* ARTHUR *that he is needed outside.*)

ARTHUR

I think they need me outside.
> (*He moves to the door.*)

72

THE GIRL

Yes, we really shouldn't have been talking during the service.
(ARTHUR *goes out of the office, closing the door behind
him. He joins* SCHLISSEL, *who is a few steps away, muttering the prayers.*)

ARTHUR

(*Shaking his head*)

What a pity, really. A lovely girl. What a pity. Now, you look
like a sensible sort of man. What is all this nonsense about demons? You really should call her father or mother or whoever it
is who is responsible for her.

SCHLISSEL

Young man, if we called her father he would come down and
take her away.

ARTHUR

Yes. That would be the point, wouldn't it?

SCHLISSEL

Then what happens to our exorcism?

ARTHUR

What exorcism?

SCHLISSEL

Listen, we've got to exorcise the dybbuk.

ARTHUR

(*Aghast*)

Exorcism!
(THE SEXTON *leans over the railing of the platform and admonishes them in a heavy whisper.*)

73

THE SEXTON

Sssshhhh!

(SCHLISSEL *promptly turns back to muttering his prayers.*
ARTHUR *stares at him with vague disbelief.*)

ARTHUR

Are you serious?
(ZITORSKY's *voice rises up loud and clear.*)

ZITORSKY

". . . And it is said, and the Lord shall be king over all the
earth; on that day shall the Lord be One, and His Name One."
(THE CONGREGATION, *which had been sitting, now stands
again.* THE SEXTON *leans over the railing and calls to the
KESSLER boys.*)

THE SEXTON

Kessler, stand up. Now is the time for your memorial prayers.
(*The two* KESSLER *boys nod, stand, and look unhappily
down at their prayer books.* HARRIS *pokes a palsied finger
onto a page to show them where to read, and the two
young men now begin to read painstakingly and with no
idea of what they are reading.*)

KESSLER BOYS

"Magnified and sanctified be His great Name in the world
which He hath created according to His will. May He establish
His kingdom in your lifetime and in your days, and in the lifetime of all the house of Israel, speedily and at a near time; and
say ye, Amen."

CONGREGATION

Amen. "Let His great Name be blessed for ever and ever."

74

KESSLER BOYS

"Blessed, praised, and glorified, exalted, extolled and honored, adored, and lauded, be the Name of the Holy One, blessed be He, beyond, yea, beyond all blessings and hymns, praises and songs, which are uttered in the world, and say ye, Amen."

CONGREGATION

Amen.

(*The front door to the synagogue bursts open and* FORE-MAN *thrusts himself in, obviously much distraught; not so distraught, however, that he doesn't automatically join in the "Amen."*)

KESSLER BOYS

"May there be abundant peace from heaven, and life for us and for all Israel; and say ye, Amen."

CONGREGATION

Amen.

KESSLER BOYS

"May he who maketh peace in his high places, make peace for us and for all Israel, and say ye, Amen."

CONGREGATION

Amen.

(*The synagogue bursts into a quick mumble of prayers, except for* SCHLISSEL, *who scurries over to* FOREMAN. FORE-MAN *stares at him, white with panic.*)

SCHLISSEL

What happened? You got lost? You took the Long Island Railroad to Atlantic Avenue Station, and you got lost in the Atlantic Avenue Station?

FOREMAN

What Atlantic Avenue Station? I couldn't even find the Long Island Railroad!

SCHLISSEL

Idiot! You are an innocent child! Really! Services are over in a minute, and I'll take you myself. (ALPER *is leaning over the railing of the platform, making obvious gestures, as if to ask what had happened. Even* ZITORSKY *looks up from his hunched position at the lectern.* SCHLISSEL *announces in a heavy whisper, as he starts to put on his coat—*) He couldn't even find the Long Island Railway Station. (ALPER *clasps his brow.* THE SEXTON *turns around to* SCHLISSEL *and admonishes him with a heavy "Ssshhh!!!"* FOREMAN *has begun walking about, mumbling the prayers by heart, automatically a part of the service again. As he passes* SCHLISSEL, *he indicates with a jerk of his head that he would like to know of the well-being of his granddaughter*) She's all right. Don't worry about her.

(FOREMAN *nods and continues mumbling his prayers. In* THE RABBI'S *office,* THE GIRL, *who has been sitting pensively, now stands, puts her coat on, goes out of the office, calmly crosses to the rear of the synagogue, and exits through the front door. Absolutely no one is aware she has gone.* THE CONGREGATION *now bursts into a loud prayer, obviously the last one of the service, since the men on the platform begin to meander off, and all those who are still wearing their phylacteries begin to strip them off, even as they say the words of the prayer.*)

CONGREGATION

"He is the Lord of the Universe, who reigned ere any creature yet was formed.

At the time when all things were made by His desire, then was
  His name proclaimed King.
And after all things shall have had an end, He alone, the dread-
  est one shall reign;
Who was, who is, and who will be in glory."

(SCHLISSEL, ALPER, ZITORSKY, *and* FOREMAN *have all rattled
quickly through this final paean, impatient to close off the
service, while the others continue the terminal recital. The
four old men form a huddled group by the front door.*)

ALL FOUR
(*Rattling it off*)
"And with my spirit, my body, also; the Lord is with me, and
I will not fear. Amen."

ALPER

Amen, what happened?

SCHLISSEL

I'm taking him myself right away.

ZITORSKY

What happened, you got lost?

FOREMAN

I asked this fellow in the street, I said: "Could you . . ."

SCHLISSEL
(*To* ALPER, *pointing to* ARTHUR)
Listen, keep an eye on that fellow there. He wants to tell the
Rabbi about the girl. All right, listen. I shall have to lead Fore-
man by the hand to Korpotchniker. All right, listen, we're going.
Good-bye. Peace be unto you.

ALPER

Take the Long Island Railroad to the Atlantic Avenue Station. Then take the Brighton train.

SCHLISSEL

Oh, for heaven's sakes. Are you presuming to tell me how to get to Williamsburg?

ALPER

All right, go already.

SCHLISSEL

(*Muttering as he leads* FOREMAN *out the door*)
The Brighton train. If we took the Brighton train, we would spend the day in Coney Island.
(*He exits with* FOREMAN, *closing the door. The rest of the* CONGREGATION *has finally come to the end of the service.*)

CONGREGATION

(*Their scattered voices rising to a coda*)
"And with my spirit, my body also; the Lord is with me, and I will not fear. Amen!"

ZITORSKY *and* ALPER

Amen!
(*There is a flurry of dispersion. The two* KESSLER *boys mumble good-byes and disappear quickly out into the street, buttoning their coats against the cold.* HARRIS, *who is slowly and tremblingly removing his phylacteries, continues slowly to dress himself again throughout the rest of the scene.* THE SEXTON *now scurries about, gathering the various phylacteries and prayer shawls and putting them back into the velvet prayer bags and then putting all the*

78

*velvet bags and prayer books back into the cardboard car-
ton they were all taken from, an activity he pursues with
his usual frenetic desperation. Only* THE RABBI *and* THE
CABALIST *continue to say a few extra prayers: "The Thir-
teen Principles of Faith," etc.* THE CABALIST *reads them sitting down, hunched over his prayer book.* ALPER *and* ZITOR-
SKY *have genuine cause for alarm concerning* ARTHUR LAN-
DAU, *for he has ambled down to the platform, where he
stands waiting for* THE RABBI *to finish his prayers. They
watch* ARTHUR *guardedly.* HARRIS *suddenly decides to be
communicative. He lifts his old face to* ALPER *and* ZITOR-
SKY.)

HARRIS

Ah, am I thirsty!

ALPER

(*Watching* ARTHUR *carefully*)

Good.

(THE RABBI, *having finished his last prayer, now turns and
starts down from the platform.* ARTHUR *steps forward to
meet him.*)

ARTHUR

Rabbi . . .

THE RABBI

(*Walking by him*)

I'll be with you in just a moment.

(*He strides directly to his office.* ALPER *leaps to intercept
him.*)

ALPER

Rabbi . . .

THE RABBI

(*Continuing into his office*)

I'll be with you in a minute, Alper. (*He goes into his office and closes the door.* ALPER *clasps his brow and shrugs.* ZITORSKY *mutters an involuntary "Oy." They both nod their heads and wait with the sufferance that is the badge of all their tribe.* ARTHUR *moves a few steps to* THE RABBI's *door and also waits. In the office,* THE RABBI *sits down—all business—and dials a number. Then he speaks into the phone*) I'd like to make a person-to-person call to Rabbi Harry Gersh in Wilmington, Delaware. The number in Wilmington is Kingswood 3-1973 . . . Thank you . . . (*He hums a snatch of the service.* ALPER *knocks lightly on the door, and, receiving no answer, opens the door and comes into the office. He stares—open-mouthed—noting the absence of* THE GIRL. *He tugs at his Vandyke beard in contemplation*) Yes, Alper?

ALPER

Well, I'll tell you, Rabbi . . . (*He scowls, a little flustered, then turns and goes out of the office*) Excuse me.

THE RABBI

(*On the phone*)

Locust 6-0932.

ALPER

(*To* ZITORSKY)

She's not there.

ZITORSKY

She's not there?

80

ALPER

I'll have to go out and look for her.

(*Frowning in contemplation,* ALPER *puts his coat on slowly and exits from the synagogue.* THE RABBI *is still on the phone. His voice rises to the pitch usually used for long-distance calls.*)

THE RABBI

Harry, how are you, this is Bernard here, I'm sorry I wasn't in last night, my wife Sylvia said it was wonderful to hear your voice after all these years, how are you, Shirley, and the kids, oh, that's wonderful, I'm glad to hear it. Harry, my wife tells me you have just gotten your first congregation and you wanted some advice since I have already been fired several times . . . Good, how much are you getting? . . . Well, five thousand isn't bad for a first congregation although I always thought out-of-town paid better. And what is it, a one-year contract? . . . Well, what kind of advice can I give you? Especially you, Harry. You are a saintly, scholarly, and truly pious man, and you have no business being a rabbi. You've got to be a go-getter, Harry, unfortunately. The synagogue I am in now is in an unbelievable state of neglect and I expect to see us in prouder premises within a year. But I've got things moving now. I've started a Youth Group, a Young Married People's Club, a Theatre Club which is putting on its first production next month, *The Man Who Came to Dinner,* I'd like you to come, Harry, bring the wife, I'm sure you'll have an entertaining evening. And let me recommend that you organize a little-league baseball team. It's a marvelous gimmick. I have sixteen boys in my Sunday School now . . . Harry, listen, what do I know about baseball? . . . Harry, let me interrupt you. How in heaven's name are you going to convey an awe of God to boys who will race out of your Hebrew classes to fly model rocket ships five hundred feet in the air exploding in three stages? To my boys, God is a retired mechanic . . . Well, I'm organizing a bazaar right now. When I hang up on you, I have to rush to the printer's to get some raffles printed, and from there I go to the Town Hall for a permit to conduct bingo games. In fact, I was so busy this morning, I almost forgot to come to the synagogue . . . (*He says gently*) Harry, with my first congregation, I also thought I was bringing the word of God. I stood up in my pulpit every Sabbath and carped at them for violating the rituals of their own religion. My congregations dwindled, and one synagogue given to my charge disappeared into a morass of mortgages. Harry, I'm afraid there are times when I don't care if they believe in God as long as they come to the synagogue . . . Of course, it's sad . . . Harry, it's been my pleasure. Have I depressed you? . . . Come and see us, Harry . . . Good luck . . . Of course. Good-bye.

> (*He hangs up, stands, starts looking around for his briefcase, and strides out into the synagogue still searching for it. He is interrupted by* ARTHUR.)

ARTHUR

Rabbi, I have to hurry off, but before I go I would like to talk to you about that girl in your office. These old men tell me she is possessed by a demon and I think they are intending to perform some kind of an exorcism. I must caution you that that girl should be treated only by competent psychiatrists and the most frightful harm might come to her if she is subjected to anything like— Look, do you know about this exorcism, because I cannot believe you would tolerate any . . .

THE RABBI

(*Who has been trying very hard to follow all this*)
I'm afraid you have me at a disadvantage.

ARTHUR

I'm talking about the girl in your office.

THE RABBI

I'm somewhat new here and don't know everybody yet by
name. Please be patient with me. Now, I take it you want to get
married.
(*For a moment* ARTHUR *briefly considers the possibility he
is not really awake.*)

ARTHUR

(*Pensively*)
This whole morning is beginning to seem absolutely . . .
Rabbi, there is a girl in your office who is insane.

THE RABBI

In my office? (THE RABBI *is suddenly distracted by* ZITORSKY,
*who has been wandering around the synagogue, looking up and
down between the rows of chairs, and is now looking into the
bathroom at the upstage end of the synagogue*) Mr. Zitorsky,
what are you doing?

ZITORSKY

(*To* ARTHUR, *who is moving quickly to* THE RABBI'S *office*)
Well, have you ever seen such a thing? The girl has vanished
into thin air.
(*He shuffles to* THE RABBI, *absolutely awe-struck by it all.*)

ARTHUR

(*Now examining the interior of* THE RABBI's *office*)
I suspect something more mundane, like simply walking out
the door.

(*He moves quickly to the front door, which now opens,
and* ALPER *returns, frowning with thought.*)

ALPER

(*To* ARTHUR)
Well, is that something or isn't it? I looked up and down, I
couldn't see her.

(ARTHUR *scowls and goes out into the street, where he
stands looking up and down.*)

THE RABBI

Mr. Zitorsky, if you will just tell me what this is all about.

ZITORSKY

(*His eyes wide with awe*)
Rabbi, Mr. Foreman brought his granddaughter down this
morning, and he said: "She is possessed by a dybbuk!" Well,
what can you say when someone tells you something like that?

THE RABBI

Oh, Mr. Foreman's granddaughter. Yes, of course, I see.

ZITORSKY

So he took us into your office where she was standing, and it
spoke to us! What an experience! You cannot imagine! The
voice of the dybbuk spoke to us. It was like a hollow echo of
eternity, and the girl's whole body was illuminated by a frame of
light! Fire flashed from her mouth. All of us were there, ask

Alper here, he'll tell you. I swear this on my soul! The girl began to rise into the air!

ALPER

Actually, Zitorsky is coloring the story a little.

ZITORSKY

(*Riveted by the marvelousness of the fantasy*)
What are you talking about? You saw it with your own eyes!

ALPER

Well, it was an experience, I must say.

THE RABBI

And the girl has gone now.

ZITORSKY

Into the air about us.

THE RABBI

And where is Mr. Foreman?

ALPER

He went to Brooklyn.

THE RABBI

What in heaven's name for?

ALPER

To see the Korpotchniker Rabbi.

THE RABBI

(*Quite impressed*)
The Korpotchniker?

85

ZITORSKY

Certainly! Maybe you don't know this, but Hirschman is his cousin.

THE RABBI

Mr. Hirschman? I have to admit I didn't know that.

ZITORSKY

Oh, sure. Listen, Hirschman is the first-born son of the original Korpotchniker.

ALPER

I am afraid we are drifting from the point.

THE RABBI

(*Frowning*)

The girl probably went home. Why don't you call the girl's home, Mr. Alper, and find out if she's there? I think you are a very close friend of the family.

ARTHUR

(*Who has come back into the synagogue*)

Well, thank God for the first rational voice I've heard today.

ALPER

(*Nodding his head sadly*)

Yes, I suppose I had better call her father.

ARTHUR

(*Buttoning his coat*)

Fine. (*Glancing at his watch*) Gentlemen, if you don't need

86

me for anything any more, I would like to get to my analyst. Good morning.
> (*He strides to the door.*)

THE RABBI

Peace be unto you.
> (ARTHUR *pauses at the front door, a little amused at the archaic greeting.*)

ARTHUR

Peace be unto you, Rabbi.
> (*He opens the door and goes out.*)

THE RABBI

Who was that fellow?

ZITORSKY

Who knows? The Sexton found him on the street.

THE RABBI

(*Buttoning his own coat*)

Well, I have to be down at the printer's. A dybbuk. Really. What an unusual thing. Is Mr. Foreman a mystical man? By the way, Mr. Alper—Mr. Zitorsky—you weren't at the meeting of the Brotherhood last night. I think you should take a more active interest in the synagogue. Did you receive an announcement of the meeting? Please come next time. (*He finds his briefcase*) Ah, there it is, good. (*He heads for the door*) I would like to know what the Korpotchniker said about this. Will you be here later today? I'll drop in. Let me know what happens. You better call the girl's family right away, Alper. Good morning. Peace be with you.

ALPER *and* ZITORSKY

Peace be with you, Rabbi.

(THE RABBI *exits. The two old men regard each other a
little balefully, and then shuffle to* THE RABBI'S *office, where*
ALPER *sits down and puts his hand on the phone, resting it
on the receiver, quite depressed by the turn of events. In
the synagogue,* THE CABALIST *is huddled in prayer, and* THE
SEXTON *has gotten a broom out and is sweeping an upstage
area. A long moment of hushed silence fills the stage.*)

ALPER

(*His hand still on the phone*)

Zitorsky, let us reason this out.

ZITORSKY

Absolutely.

ALPER

(*The Talmudic scholar*)

If I call the girl's home, there are two possibilities. Either she
is home or she is not home. If she is home, why call? If she is not
home, then there are two possibilities. Either her father has already called the police, or he has not called the police. If he has
already called the police, then we are wasting a telephone call. If
he has not called the police, he will call them. If he calls the
police, then there are two possibilities. Either they will take the
matter seriously or they will not. If they don't take the matter
seriously, why bother calling them? If they take the matter seriously, they will rush down here to find out what we already
know, so what gain will have been made? Nothing. Have I
reasoned well, Zitorsky?

ZITORSKY

You have reasoned well.

ALPER

Between you and me, Zitorsky, how many people are there on the streets at this hour that we couldn't spot the girl in a minute? Why should we trouble the immense machinery of the law? We'll go out and find the girl ourselves.

(*They are both up in a minute, buttoning their coats and hurrying to the front door, where they pause.*)

ZITORSKY

(*Regarding* ALPER *with awe*)

Alper, what a rogue you are!

(ALPER *accepts the compliment graciously, and they both dart out into the street. Then, out of the hollow hush of the stage,* THE CABALIST'S *voice rises into a lovely chant as he rocks back and forth, his eyes closed in religious ecstasy.*)

THE CABALIST

(*Singing slowly and with profound conviction*)

"I believe with perfect faith in the coming of the Messiah, and
   though he tarry, I will wait daily for his coming.
I believe with perfect faith that there will be a resurrection of the
   dead
 at the time when it shall please the Creator,
 blessed be His name,
 and exalted the remembrance of him for ever and ever."

(*The front door opens, and* THE GIRL *comes rushing in, holding a beautifully bound leather book. She looks quickly around the synagogue, now empty except for* THE SEXTON *and* THE CABALIST, *and then hurries to* THE RABBI'S *office, which is of course also empty. A kind of panic*) *sweeps over her, and she rushes out into the synagogue again, to* THE SEXTON.)

THE GIRL

Mr. Bleyer, the young man that was here, do you know . . . (*She whirls as the front door opens behind her and* ARTHUR *comes in. We have the feeling he also has been, if not running, at least walking very quickly. He and* THE GIRL *stare at each other for a moment. Then she says to him—*) I went home to get this book for you. I wanted you to have this book I told you about.

ARTHUR

(*Quietly*)

I just simply couldn't go till I knew you were all right.

(*For a moment they stand poised, staring at each other. Then she sweeps across the stage and flings herself into his arms.*)

THE GIRL

(*Crying out*)

Oh, I love you. I love you. I love you . . .

(*They stand, locked in embrace.* THE CABALIST's *voice rises again in a deeply primitive chant, exquisite in its atavistic ardor.*)

THE CABALIST

"For Thy salvation I hope, O Lord! I hope, O Lord, for Thy salvation. O Lord, for Thy salvation I hope!

For Thy salvation I hope, O Lord! I hope, O Lord, for Thy salvation! O Lord, for Thy salvation I hope!"

The Curtain Falls

SCENE 2

It is now several hours later. A silent, dozing quiet has settled over the synagogue. Indeed, THE CABALIST *has dozed off* over a thick tome at the upstage desk on the far side of the altar, *his shawl-enshrouded head lying on his book.* THE GIRL, *too, is napping, curled up in the worn leather armchair in* THE RABBI'S *office.* THE SEXTON *is sitting like a cobbler on a chair stage left.* ALPER *and* ZITORSKY *sit drowsily on two wooden chairs, center stage. Only* ARTHUR *moves restlessly around the synagogue. He looks into* THE RABBI'S *office, checking on* THE GIRL, *studies her sleeping sweetness, somehow deeply troubled. All is still, all is quiet.*

In the synagogue, THE CABALIST *awakens suddenly and sits bolt upright, as if he has just had the most bizarre dream. He stares wide-eyed at the wall in front of him. He rises, and moves slowly downstage, his face a study in quiet awe. Apparently, he has had a profoundly moving dream, and he puts his hand to his brow as if to keep his thoughts from tumbling out. An expression of exaltation spreads across his wan, lined, bearded old face. His eyes are wide with terror.*

THE CABALIST

(*Whispering in awe*)

"Blessed be the Lord. Blessed be the Lord. Blessed be the Lord." (*He stands now almost at the footlights, staring out over the audience, his face illuminated with ecstasy. He cries out*)

91

Praise ye the Lord! Hallelujah! Praise ye the Lord! Hallelujah! It is good to sing praises unto our God; for it is pleasant and praise is seemly. Praise ye the Lord! Hallelujah! (ALPER *has watched* THE CABALIST *with drowsy interest.* THE CABALIST *turns and stares at him*) My dear friends, my dear, dear friends . . . (*Tears fill his old eyes, and his mouth works without saying anything for a moment.*)

ALPER

Are you all right, Hirschman?

THE CABALIST

(*Awed by an inner wonder*)

I was studying the codification of the Law, especially those paragraphs beginning with the letters of my father's name—because today is my father's day of memorial. I have brought some honey cake here, in my father's memory. I have it somewhere in a paper bag. Where did I put it? I brought it here last night. It is somewhere around—and as I studied, I dozed off and my head fell upon the Book of Mishna. Oh, my dear friends, I have prayed to the Lord to send me a dream, and He has sent me a dream. I dreamt that I was bathing in a pool of the clearest mountain water. And a man of great posture appeared on the bank, and he said to me: "Rabbi, give me your blessing, for I go to make a journey." And I looked closely on the man, and it was the face of my father. And I said unto him: "My father, why do you call me Rabbi? For did I not lustfully throw away the white fringed shawl of the rabbinate and did I not mock the Lord to thy face? And have I not spent my life in prayer and penitence so that I might cleanse my soul?" And my father smiled upon me, and his bearded face glowed with

92

gentleness, and he said unto me: "Rise from your bath, my son, and put upon you these robes of white linen which I have arrayed for you. For thy soul is cleansed and thou hast found a seat among the righteous. And the countenance of the Lord doth smile upon thee this day. So rise and rejoice and dance in the Holy Place. For thine is eternal peace and thou art among the righteous." Thus was the dream that I dreamt as my head lay on the Book of Mishna. (*He lifts his head and stares upward*) The Lord shall reign for ever. Thy God, O Zion, unto all generations. Praise ye the Lord. Hallelujah! (*He stares distractedly around him*) Where is the wine, Sexton? The wine! There was a fine new bottle on Friday! I have been given a seat among the righteous! For this day have I lived and fasted! I have been absolved! Hallelujah! Hallelujah!— Ah, the cakes! Here! Good!—(*He is beginning to laugh*) I shall dance before the Holy Ark! Sexton! Sexton! Distribute the macaroons that all may share this exalted day! The Lord hath sent me a sign, and the face of my father smiled upon me!

> (*As abruptly as he had begun to laugh he begins to sob in the effusion of his joy. He sinks onto a chair and cries unashamedly.*)

ALPER

My dear Hirschman, how delighted we are for you.

THE SEXTON

(*Offering some honey cake to* ZITORSKY)
You want some cake there, Zitorsky?

ZITORSKY

I'll have a little wine too as long as we're having a party.

(THE SEXTON *scurries off to the lectern, the bottom of which is a cabinet containing various sacramental things and wine.*)

ARTHUR

(*Who has been watching all this, rather taken by it*)
What happened?

ALPER

Mr. Hirschman has received a sign from God. His father has forgiven him, and his soul has been cleansed.

ARTHUR

That's wonderful.

ZITORSKY

(*To* THE SEXTON, *now pouring wine from a decanter*)
I'll tell you, Bleyer, if you have a little whiskey, I prefer that. Wine makes me dizzy.

THE SEXTON

Where would I get whiskey? This is a synagogue, not a saloon.

ZITORSKY

(*Taking his glass of wine*)
Happiness, Hirschman.

ALPER

Some wine for our young friend here. (*To* ARTHUR) Will you join Mr. Hirschman in his moment of exaltation?

ARTHUR

Yes, of course.
(THE SEXTON, *who is pouring the wine and sipping a glass of his own as he pours, has begun to hum a gay Chassidic tune. He hands* ARTHUR *his glass.*)

ZITORSKY

(*Handing his glass back for a refill*)
Oh, will Schlissel eat his heart out when he finds out he is missing a party.

ALPER

(*Making a toast*)
Rabbi Israel, son of Isaac, I think it is fitting we use your rabbinical title—we bow in reverence to you.

THE CABALIST

(*Deeply touched*)
My dear, dear friends, I cannot describe to you my happiness.

ZITORSKY

There hasn't been a party here since that boy's confirmation last month. Wasn't that a skimpy feast for a confirmation? Another glass, please, Sexton. Oh, I'm beginning to sweat. Some confirmation party that was! The boy's father does a nice business in real estate and all he brings down is a few pieces of sponge cake and one bottle of whiskey. One bottle of whiskey for fifty people! As much whiskey as I had couldn't even cure a toothache. Oh, boy, am I getting dizzy. When I was a boy, I could drink a whole jar of potato cider. You remember that potato cider we used to have in Europe? It could kill a horse. Oh, boy, what kind of wine is that? My legs are like rubber already.

(ZITORSKY *suddenly stamps his foot and executes a few brief Chassidic dance steps.*)

ALPER

This is not bad wine, you know. A pleasant bouquet.

ZITORSKY

(*Wavering over to* ARTHUR)

Have a piece of cake, young man. What does it say in the Bible? "Go eat your food with gladness and drink your wine with a happy mind?" Give the boy another glass.

ARTHUR

(*Smiling*)

Thank you. I'm still working on this one.

(THE CABALIST *suddenly raises his head and bursts into a gay Chassidic chant.*)

THE CABALIST

(*Bursting into song*)

"Light is sown,
  sown for the righteous,
  and joy for the upright,
  the upright in heart.
  Oh,
  light is sown,
  sown for the righteous . . ."

ZITORSKY

(*Gaily joining in*)

"and joy for the upright,
the upright in heart.
Oh!"

(THE CABALIST *and* ZITORSKY *take each other's shoulders and begin to dance in the formless Chassidic pattern. They are in wonderful spirits*)

"Light is sown,
sown for the righteous ..."

(THE SEXTON *and* ALPER *join in, clapping their hands and eventually joining the dance so that the four old Jews form a small ring, their arms around each other's shoulders, their old feet kicking exuberantly as they stamp about in a sort of circular pattern.*)

ALL

"... and joy for the upright,
the upright in heart."
Oh!

Light is sown,
sown for the righteous,
and joy for the upright,
the upright in heart.

(*Round and round they stomp and shuffle, singing out lustily, sweat forming in beads on their brows. The words are repeated over and over again until they degenerate, from the shortness of breath of the singers, into a "Bi-bu-bu-bi-bi-bi-bi-bi-bi-bibibi."* ARTHUR *watches, delighted.*

Finally, ALPER, *gasping for breath, breaks out of the ring and staggers to a chair.*)

THE CABALIST

A good sixty years I haven't danced! Oh, enough! Enough! My heart feels as if it will explode!
(*He staggers, laughing, from the small ring of dancers and sits down, gasping for air.*)

ALPER

Some more wine, Hirschman?

THE CABALIST

(*Gasping happily*)

Oh!
(ZITORSKY *looks up, noticing* THE GIRL, *who, awakened by the romping, has sidled out into the synagogue and has been watching the gaiety with delight.* ZITORSKY *eyes her wickedly for a moment; then advances on her, his arm outstretched, quite the old cock-of-the-walk.*)

ZITORSKY

Bi-bi-bi-bi-bi-bi-bi . . .
(*He seizes her in his arms and begins to twirl around, much to her delight. She dances with him, her skirts whirling and her feet twinkling, laughing at the sheer physical excitement of it all.* ZITORSKY *supplies the music, a gay chant, the lyrics of which consist of: "Bi-bi-bi-bi-bi-bi-bi-bi . . .")*

98

THE CABALIST

The last time I danced was on the occasion of the last Day of the Holiday of Tabernacles in 1896. I was seventeen years old. (*A sudden frightened frown sweeps across his face. He mutters*) Take heed for the girl, for the dybbuk will be upon her soon.

ALPER

(Leaning to him)

What did you say, Israel son of Isaac?

(THE CABALIST *turns to* THE GIRL *dancing with* ZITORSKY, *and stares at her.*)

THE CABALIST

Let the girl rest, Zitorsky, for she struggles with the dybbuk. Behold. (THE GIRL *has indeed broken away from* ZITORSKY *and has begun an improvised dance of her own. The gaiety is gone from her face and is replaced by a sullen lasciviousness. The dance she does is a patently provocative one. She dances slowly at first, and then with increasing abandon and wantonness.* ZITORSKY *recoils in horror.* THE GIRL *begins to stamp her feet and to whirl more and more wildly. Her eyes grow bold and flashing and she begins to shout old Gypsy words, a mongrel Russian, Oriental in intonation.* THE CABALIST *now slowly moves to* THE GIRL, *who, when she becomes aware of his coming close, abruptly stops her dance and stands stock-still, her face a mask of extravagant pain.* THE CABALIST *regards her gently*) Lie down, my child, and rest.

(*At this quiet suggestion,* THE GIRL *begins to sway as if she is about to faint.*)

THE GIRL
(*Barely audible*)

I feel so faint, so faint.
(*She sinks slowly to the floor, not quite in a swoon, but on the verge.* ARTHUR *races to her side.*)

ARTHUR

Do we have any water here?

ALPER

Wine would be better. Sexton, give her some wine.
(THE SEXTON *hurries with someone's glass.*)

ARTHUR
(*Holding* THE GIRL's *head*)

Is she a sickly girl?

ALPER
(*Bending over them*)

She was never sick a day in her life.

THE SEXTON

Here's the wine.

ZITORSKY
(*To* THE SEXTON)

Did I tell you? Did I tell you?

THE GIRL

I feel so faint. I feel so faint.

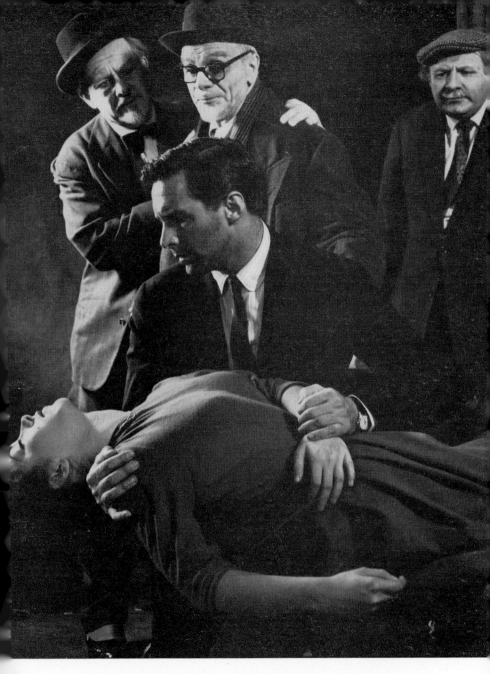

Background: George Voskovec, Jacob Ben-Ami, and Lou Jacobi, as ALPER, FOREMAN, and SCHLISSEL. *Foreground:* Risa Schwartz and Donald Harron, as THE GIRL and ARTHUR LANDAU

ARTHUR

(*Bringing the glass of wine to her lips*)

Sip some of this.

THE GIRL

(*Murmuring*)

Save me . . . save me . . .

THE CABALIST

The dybbuk weakens her. I have seen this once before.

THE SEXTON

(*To* ZITORSKY)

When you told me about this dybbuk, I didn't believe you.

ZITORSKY

So did I tell you right?

THE SEXTON

Oh, boy.

ARTHUR

Help me get her onto the chair in there.

ALPER

Yes, of course.

THE SEXTON

Here, let me help a little.

(*Between them, they manage to get* THE GIRL *up and walk her slowly to* THE RABBI's *office, where they gently help her lie down on the leather sofa.*)

THE CABALIST

(*To* ZITORSKY)

They haven't heard from Mr. Foreman yet?

ZITORSKY

No, we're waiting.

THE CABALIST

(*Frowning*)

It is not that far to Williamsburg. Well, the girl will sleep now.
(*He walks slowly to the door of* THE RABBI'S *office, followed by a wary* ZITORSKY. ALPER *returns to the synagogue
proper to join the other old men, and, for the briefest of
moments,* ARTHUR *finds himself alone with* THE GIRL,
*holding her head gently in his arms. Suddenly he kisses
her brow and lightly strokes her hair. He rises quickly as
the others return.*)

ARTHUR

I think she's fallen asleep.

ALPER

Thank heavens for that.

ARTHUR

Look, I'm going to call her family. She may be quite ill. I
think we'd all feel a lot better if she were in the hands of a doctor.
If one of you will just give me her home telephone number . . .
(*Just a little annoyed, for nobody answers him*) Please, gentlemen, I really don't think it's wise to pursue this nonsense any
longer.

THE CABALIST

It is not nonsense. I do not speak of dybbuks casually. As a young man, I saw hundreds of people come to my father claiming to be possessed, but, of all these, only two were true dybbuks. Of these two, one was a girl very much like this poor girl, and, even before the black candles and the ram's horn could be brought for the exorcism, she sank down onto the earth and died. I tell you this girl is possessed, and she will die, clutching at her throat and screaming for redemption unless the dybbuk is exorcised. (*He stares at the others and nods his head*) She will die. Wake the girl. I will take her to the Korpotchniker myself.

ALPER

Zitorsky, wake the girl. I will get her coat. Sexton, call a taxicab for Rabbi Israel. (ALPER, *who had been reaching for* THE GIRL's *coat, is stayed by* ARTHUR. *He looks up at the young man*) Young man, what are you doing?

ARTHUR

Mr. Alper, the girl is sick. There may be something seriously wrong with her.

ALPER

Young man, Rabbi Israel says she is dying.

ARTHUR

Well, in that case certainly, let me have her home telephone number.

ALPER

(*Striding into* THE RABBI's *office*)
You are presuming in matters that are no concern of yours.

ARTHUR

(*Following*)

They are as much my concern as they are yours. I have grown quite fond of this girl. I want her returned to the proper authorities, right now. If necessary, I shall call a policeman. Now, let's have no more nonsense.

(ALPER *sinks down behind the desk, glowering. A moment of silence fills the room. Then* THE CABALIST, *who has been standing in the rear of the office and watching with quiet interest, says—*)

THE CABALIST

The young man doesn't believe in dybbuks?

ARTHUR

I'm afraid not. I think you are all behaving like madmen.

(THE CABALIST *considers this answer for a moment.*)

THE CABALIST

I will tell you an old Chassidic parable. A deaf man passed by a house in which a wedding party was going on. He looked in the window and saw all the people there dancing and cavorting, leaping about and laughing. However, since the man was deaf and could not hear the music of the fiddlers, he said to himself: "Ah, this must be a madhouse." Young man, because you are deaf, must it follow that we are lunatics?

ARTHUR

You are quite right. I did not mean to mock your beliefs, and I apologize for it. However, I am going to call the girl's father, and, if he wants to have the girl exorcised, that's his business.

(He sits down behind the desk, puts his hand on the receiver, and looks up at ALPER*)* Well?

THE CABALIST

Give him the number, Mr. Alper. (ALPER *fishes an old address book out of his vest pocket, thumbs through the pages, and hands the open book to* ARTHUR, *who begins to dial*) There is no one home in the girl's house. Her father, who wishes only to forget about the girl, has gone to his shop in the city, and, at this moment, is overeating at his lunch in a dairy restaurant. The stepmother has taken the younger children to her sister's. The girl's doctor has called the police and has gone about his rounds, and the police are diffidently riding up and down the streets of the community, looking for an old Jew and his granddaughter. (ARTHUR *says nothing, but simply waits for an answer to his ring.* THE CABALIST *sits down on the arm of the couch to contemplate. At last he says—*) I cannot understand why this young man does not believe in dybbuks.

ALPER

It is symptomatic of the current generation, Rabbi Israel, to be utterly disillusioned. Historically speaking, an era of prosperity following an era of hard times usually produces a number of despairing and quietistic philosophies, for the now prosperous people have found out they are just as unhappy as when they were poor. Thus when an intelligent man of such a generation discovers that two television sets have no more meaning than one or that he gets along no better with his wife in a suburban house than he did in their small city flat, he arrives at the natural assumption that life is utterly meaningless.

THE CABALIST

What an unhappy state of affairs.
(ARTHUR *returns the receiver to its cradle*.)

ARTHUR
(*Muttering*)
Nobody home.

THE CABALIST
(*To* ARTHUR)
Is that true, young man, that you believe in absolutely nothing?

ARTHUR
Not a damn thing.

THE CABALIST
There is no truth, no beauty, no infinity, no known, no unknown.

ARTHUR
Precisely.

THE CABALIST
Young man, you are a fool.

ARTHUR
Really. I have been reading your book—the Book of Zohar. I am sure it has lost much in the translation, but, sir, any disciple of this abracadabra is presuming when he calls anyone else a fool.

(ARTHUR *produces from his jacket the book* THE GIRL *gave him, and extends it to* THE CABALIST, *who accepts it, frowning.*)

THE CABALIST

You have been reading the Book of Zohar. Dear young man, one does not read the Book of Zohar, leaf through its pages, and make marginal notes. I have entombed myself in this slim volume for sixty years, raw with vulnerability to its hidden mysteries, and have sensed only a glimpse of its passion. Behind every letter of every word lies a locked image, and behind every image a sparkle of light of the ineffable brilliance of Infinity. But the concept of the Inexpressible Unknown is inconceivable to you. For you are a man possessed by the Tangible. If you cannot touch it with your fingers, it simply does not exist. Indeed, that will be the epithet of your generation—that you took everything for granted and believed in nothing. It is a very little piece of life that we know. How shall I say it? I suggest it is wiser to believe in dybbuks than in nothing at all.

ARTHUR

Mr. Hirschman, a good psychiatrist—even a poor one—could strip your beliefs in ten minutes. You may think of yourself as a man with a God, but I see you as a man obsessed with guilt who has invented a God so he can be forgiven. You have invented it all—the guilt, God, forgiveness, the whole world, dybbuks, love, passion, fulfillment—the whole fantastic mess of pottage—because it is unbearable for you to bear the pain of insignificance. None of these things exist. You've made them all up. The fact is, I have half a mind to let you go through with this exorcism, for, after all the trumpetings of rams' horns and the bellowing of incantations and after the girl falls in a swoon on the floor—I assure you, she will rise up again as demented as she ever was, and I wonder what bizarre rationale and mystique you will expound to explain all that. Now, if the disputation is at an end, I am going to call the police.

(*He picks up the receiver again and dials the operator.*)

ALPER

Well, what can one say to such bitterness?

THE CABALIST

(*Shrugs*)

One can only say that the young man has very little regard for psychiatrists.

(*The front door to the synagogue bursts open, and* FORE-MAN *and* SCHLISSEL *come hurtling in, breathing heavily and in a state of absolute confusion.* ALPER *darts out into the synagogue proper and stares at them.*)

SCHLISSEL

Oh, thank God, the synagogue is still here!

ALPER

Well?

SCHLISSEL

(*He can hardly talk, he is so out of breath*)
Well, what?

ALPER

What did the Korpotchniker say?

SCHLISSEL

Who knows?! Who saw the Korpotchniker?! We've been riding in subways for four hours! Back and forth, in this train, in that train! I am convinced there is no such place as Williamsburg and there is no such person as the Korpotchniker Rabbi! I tell you, twice we got off at two different stations, just to see daylight, and, as God is my witness, both times we were in New Jersey!

FOREMAN

Oh, I tell you, I am sick from driving so much.

ALPER

Idiot! You didn't take the Brighton train!

SCHLISSEL

We took the Brighton train! (*He waves both arms in a gesture of final frustration*) We took all the trains! I haven't had a bite to eat all morning. Don't tell me about Brighton trains! Don't tell me about anything! Leave me alone, and the devil take your whole capitalist economy! (ZITORSKY, THE SEXTON *and* THE CABALIST *have all come out to see what the noise is all about. Even* ARTHUR *is standing in the office doorway, listening to all this*) We asked this person, we asked that person. This person said that train. That person said this train. We went to a policeman. He puts us on a train. The conductor comes in, says: "Last stop." We get out. As God is my witness, New Jersey. We get back on that train. The conductor says: "Get off next station and take the other train." We get off the next station and take the other train. A man says: "Last stop." We get out. New Jersey! (*In* THE RABBI'S *office,* THE GIRL *suddenly sits bolt upright,*

*her eyes clenched tight in pain, screaming terribly, her
voice shrill with anguish.*)

FOREMAN

(*Racing to her side*)

Oh, my God! Evelyn! Evelyn! What is it?!

(THE GIRL *clutches at her throat and screams.*)

THE GIRL

Save me! Save me! Save me!

(ZITORSKY *and* THE SEXTON *begin to mutter rapid prayers
under their breath.*)

ALPER

(*Putting his arm around* FOREMAN)

David, she's very ill. We think she may be dying.

(ARTHUR *has raced to* THE GIRL. *He sits on the couch beside
her and takes her in his arms.*)

ARTHUR

Call a doctor.

FOREMAN

(*In panic, to* ALPER)

He says I should call a doctor.

(ARTHUR *puts his hand to his brow and shakes his head as
if to clear it of shock and confusion.*)

ALPER

(*Crossing to* THE CABALIST)

Save her, Rabbi Israel. You have had your sign from God.
You are among the righteous.

(ARTHUR *turns slowly and regards the silent betallithed form of the little* CABALIST.)

ARTHUR
(*To* THE CABALIST, *his voice cracking under emotions he was unaware he still had*)

For God's sakes, perform your exorcism or whatever has to be done. I think she's dying.

(THE CABALIST *regards* ARTHUR *for a moment with the profoundest gentleness. Then he turns and, with an authoritative voice, instructs* THE SEXTON.)

THE CABALIST
Sexton, we shall need black candles, the ram's horn, prayer shawls of white wool, and there shall be ten Jews for a quorum to witness before God this awesome ceremony.

THE SEXTON
Just plain black candles?

THE CABALIST
Just plain black candles.

(THE SEXTON *is already hurrying into his coat.* ALPER *moves quietly up to* FOREMAN *standing in the office doorway, and touches his old friend's shoulder in a gesture of awe and compassion.* FOREMAN, *at the touch, begins to cry and buries his shaking old head on his friend's shoulder.* ALPER *embraces him.*)

ZITORSKY
(*In the synagogue, to* SCHLISSEL)

I am absolutely shaking—shaking.

(ARTHUR, *having somewhat recovered his self-control, sinks down behind the desk, frowning, confused by all that is going on, and moved by a complex of feeling he cannot understand at all.*)

The Curtain Falls

ACT THREE

ACT THREE

Half an hour later.

At rise, THE GIRL *is sitting in* THE RABBI'S *office, perched on the couch, nervous, frightened, staring down at her restlessly twisting fingers.* FOREMAN *sits behind* THE RABBI'S *desk, wrapped in his own troubled thoughts. He wears over his suit a long white prayer shawl with thick black stripes, like that worn by* THE CABALIST *throughout the play.*

Indeed, all the men now wear these ankle-length white prayer shawls, except ARTHUR, *who, at rise, is also in* THE RABBI'S *office, deep in thought.*

THE CABALIST *stands downstage left, his prayer shawl hooded over his head; he is leafing through a volume, preparing the prayers for the exorcism.*

THE SEXTON *is standing by the wall phone, the receiver cradled to his ear, waiting for an answer to a call he has just put in. He is more or less surrounded by* ALPER, SCHLISSEL, *and* ZITORSKY.

ZITORSKY

How about Milsky the butcher?

ALPER

Milsky wouldn't come. Ever since they gave the seat by the East Wall to Kornblum, Milsky said he wouldn't set foot in this synagogue again. Every synagogue I have belonged to, there have always been two kosher butchers who get into a fight over who gets the favored seat by the East Wall during the High Holy Days, and the one who doesn't abandons the congregation in a fury, and the one who does always seems to die before the next High Holy Days.

SCHLISSEL

Kornblum the butcher died? I didn't know Kornblum died.

ALPER

Sure. Kornblum died four years ago.

SCHLISSEL

Well, he had lousy meat, believe me, may his soul rest in peace.
(THE SEXTON *has hung up, recouped his dime, reinserted it, and is dialing again.*)

ZITORSKY

(*To* THE SEXTON)

No answer?
(THE SEXTON *shakes his head.*)

THE SEXTON

I'm calling Harris.

SCHLISSEL

Harris? You tell an eighty-two-year-old man to come down and make a tenth for an exorcism, and he'll have a heart attack talking on the phone with you.

THE SEXTON

(*Dialing*)

Well, what else am I to do? It is hard enough to assemble ten

116

Jews under the best of circumstances, but in the middle of the afternoon on a Thursday it is an absolute nightmare. Aronowitz is in Miami. Klein the furrier is at his job in Manhattan. It is a workday today. Who shall I call? (*He waits for someone to answer*) There are many things that I have to do. The tapestries on the Ark, as you see, are faded and need needlework, and the candelabras and silver goblet for the saying of the Sabbath benediction are tarnished and dull. But every second of my day seems to be taken up with an incessant search for ten Jews . . . (*On the phone*) Hello, Harris. Harris, this is Bleyer the Sexton. We need you badly down here in the synagogue for a quorum . . . If I told you why, you wouldn't come . . . All right, I'll tell you, but, in God's name, don't tell another soul, not even your daughter-in-law . . .

SCHLISSEL

My daughter-in-law, may she grow like an onion with her head in the ground.

THE SEXTON
(*On the phone*)

Hirschman is going to exorcise a dybbuk from Foreman's granddaughter . . . I said, Hirschman is . . . A dybbuk That's right, a dybbuk . . . Right here in Mineola . . . That's right. Why should Mineola be exempt from dybbuks?

ALPER
(*Thinking of names*)

There used to be a boy came down here every morning, about eight, nine years ago—a devout boy with forelocks and side-curls—a pale boy, who was studying to be a rabbi at the seminary.

THE SEXTON

(*On the phone*)

Harris, this is not a joke.

SCHLISSEL

Chwatkin.

ALPER

That's right, Chwatkin. That was the boy's name. Chwatkin. Maybe we could call him. Does he still live in the community?

SCHLISSEL

He's a big television actor. He's on television all the time. Pinky Sims. He's an actor.

ZITORSKY

Pinky Sims? That's a name for a rabbinical student?

THE SEXTON

Put on your sweater and come down.

ALPER

(*To* THE SEXTON, *who has just hung up*)

So Harris is coming?

THE SEXTON

Yes, he's coming. So with Harris, that makes eight, and I am frankly at the end of my resources. I don't know who else to call.

ALPER

This is terrible. Really. God manifests Himself in our little synagogue, and we can't even find ten Jews to say hello.

THE SEXTON

I shall have to go out in the street and get two strangers. (*Put-*

ting on his coat) Well, I don't look forward to this at all. I will have to stop people on the street, ask them if they are Jewish—which is bad enough—and then explain to them I wish them to attend the exorcism of a dybbuk—I mean, surely you can see the futility of it.

ALPER

(*To* THE CABALIST, *who is crossing now en route to the office*)
We can only get eight. A disgrace. Really. We shall not have the exorcism for lack of two Jews.

THE SEXTON

(*On his way out*)

All right, I'm going.
(*He exits.*)

ZITORSKY

(*To* SCHLISSEL)

In those days when I was deceiving my wife, I used to tell her I was entertaining out-of-town buyers. I once told her I was entertaining out-of-town buyers every night for almost three weeks. It was a foolhardy thing to do because even my wife could tell business was not that good. So one night she came down to my loft on Thirty-Sixth Street and walked in and caught me with—well, I'm sure I've told you this story before.

SCHLISSEL

Many times.
(THE CABALIST *enters the office. Upon his entrance,* THE GIRL *stands abruptly, obviously deeply disturbed and barely in control of herself. She turns from* THE CABALIST *and shades her eyes with her hand to hide her terror.* FOREMAN *looks up briefly. He seems to be in a state of shock.*

119

THE CABALIST *sits down on the couch, letting his heavy prayer shawl fall back on his shoulders, and studies his hands folded patiently between his knees. After a moment, he speaks.)*

THE CABALIST

(Quietly)

Dybbuk, I am Israel son of Isaac. My father was Isaac son of Asher, and I wear his fringed shawl on my shoulders as I talk to you. (*Upon these words,* THE GIRL *suddenly contorts her form, as if seized by a violent cramp. She clutches her stomach and bends low, and soft sobs begin to come out of her*) Reveal yourself to me.

THE GIRL

(In the voice of the dybbuk)

I am Hannah Luchinsky.

(In the synagogue, ALPER, SCHLISSEL, *and* ZITORSKY *begin to edge—quite frightened—to the open office door.* AR-THUR *watches from his seat behind* THE RABBI'S *desk.)*

THE CABALIST

Why do you possess this girl's body?

THE GIRL

(Twisting and contorting; in the voice of the dybbuk)

My soul was lost at sea, and there is no one to say the prayers for the dead over me.

THE CABALIST

I will strike a bargain with you. Leave this girl's body through her smallest finger, doing her no damage, not even a scratch, and I shall sit on wood for you for the First Seven Days of Mourning and shall plead for your soul for the First Thirty Days and shall say the prayers for the dead over you three times a day for the Eleven Months and light the Memorial Lamp each year upon the occasion of your death. I ask you to leave this girl's body.

(THE GIRL *laughs quietly.*)

THE GIRL

(*In the voice of the dybbuk*)

You give me short weight, for you will yourself be dead before the prayers for the new moon.

(*In the office doorway, the three old men shudder.* FORE-MAN *looks up slowly.* THE CABALIST *closes his eyes.*)

THE CABALIST

(*Quietly*)

How do you know this?

THE GIRL

(*In the voice of the dybbuk*)

Your soul will fly straight to the Heavenly Gates and you will be embraced by the Archangel Mihoel.

THE CABALIST

Then I enjoin the Angel of Death to speed his way. Dybbuk, I order you to leave the body of this girl.

(THE GIRL's *face suddenly flashes with malevolence.*)

THE GIRL

(*In the voice of the dybbuk, shouting*)

No! I seek vengeance for these forty years of limbo! I was be-trayed in my youth and driven to the Evil Impulse against my will! I have suffered beyond belief, and my spirit has lived in dunghills and in piles of ashes, and I demand the soul of David

121

son of Abram be cast through Gilgul for the space of forty years times ten to gasp for air in the sea in which I drowned . . .

FOREMAN

(*Standing in terror*)

No! No!

THE GIRL

(*In the voice of the dybbuk*)

. . . so that my soul may have peace! A soul for a soul! That is my bargain.

FOREMAN

(*Shouting*)

Let it be then! Leave my granddaughter in peace and I will give my soul in exchange.

THE CABALIST

(*With ringing authority*)

The disposition of David son of Abram's soul will not be decided here. It's fall and ascent has been ordained by the second universe of angels. The bargain cannot be struck! Dybbuk, hear me. I order you to leave the body of this girl through her smallest finger, causing her no pain nor damage, and I give you my word, prayers will be said over you in full measure. But if you abjure these words, then must I proceed against you with malediction and anathema.

THE GIRL

(*Laughs*)

Raise not thy mighty arm against me, for it has no fear for me. A soul for a soul. That is my bargain.

(THE GIRL *suddenly begins to sob.*)

George Voskovec, Jacob Ben-Ami, Lou Jacobi, Arnold Marlé and
Risa Schwartz, as ALPER, FOREMAN, SCHLISSEL, THE CABALIST
and THE GIRL

THE CABALIST

(*To* ALPER)

We shall have to prepare for the exorcism.

ALPER

I thought that would be the case.

THE GIRL

(*Sitting down on the couch, frightened, in her own voice*)
I am so afraid.

FOREMAN

There is nothing to fear. It will all be over in a minute, like having a tooth pulled, and you will walk out of here a cheerful child.

SCHLISSEL

(*Ambling back into the synagogue proper with* ZITORSKY *and* ALPER)

I tell you, I'd feel a lot better if the Korpotchniker was doing this. If you are going to have a tooth pulled, at least let it be by a qualified dentist.

ZITORSKY

I thought Hirschman handled himself very well with that dybbuk.

SCHLISSEL

(*To* ALPER *and* ZITORSKY)

If I tell you all something, promise you will never throw it back in my face.

ZITORSKY

What?

SCHLISSEL

I am beginning to believe she is really possessed by a dybbuk.

ZITORSKY

I'm beginning to get used to the whole thing.

(THE CABALIST *has stood and moved upstage to the rear wall of the synagogue, where he stands in meditation.* FOREMAN *is sitting again, somewhat numb, beside his granddaughter. After a moment,* THE GIRL *speaks.*)

THE GIRL

I am very frightened, Arthur.

ARTHUR

(*Rises*)

Well, I spoke to my analyst, as you know, and he said he didn't think this exorcism was a bad idea at all. The point is, if you really do believe you are possessed by a dybbuk . . .

THE GIRL

Oh, I do.

ARTHUR

Well, then, he feels this exorcism might be a good form of shock treatment that will make you more responsive to psychiatric therapy and open the door to an eventual cure. Mr. Hirschman assures me it is a painless ceremony. So you really have nothing to be frightened of.

THE GIRL

Will you be here?

ARTHUR

Of course. Did you think I wouldn't?

124

(FOREMAN *moves slowly out into the synagogue, as if to ask something of* THE CABALIST.)

THE GIRL

I always sense flight in you.

ARTHUR

Really.

THE GIRL

You are always taking to your heels, Arthur. Especially in moments like now when you want to be tender. I know that you love me or I couldn't be so happy with you, but the whole idea of love seems to terrify you, and you keep racing off to distant detachments. I feel that if I reached out for your cheek now, you would turn your head or, in some silent way, clang the iron gates shut on me. You have some strange dybbuk all of your own, some sad little turnkey, who drifts about inside of you, locking up all the little doors, and saying, "You are dead. You are dead." You do love me, Arthur. I know that.

ARTHUR

(*Gently*)
I wish you well, Evelyn. We can at least say that.

THE GIRL

I love you. I want so very much to be your wife. (*She stares at him, her face glowing with love. She says quietly*) I will make you a good home, Arthur. You will be very happy with me. (*He regards her for a moment, caught by her wonder. He reaches forward and lightly touches her cheek. She cannot take her eyes from him*) I adore you, Arthur.

ARTHUR

(*With deep gentleness*)

You are quite mad.

(*They look at each other.* ARTHUR *stands.*)

THE GIRL

You think our getting married is impractical.

ARTHUR

Yes, I would say it was at the least impractical.

THE GIRL

Because I am insane and you are suicidal.

ARTHUR

I do think those are two reasons to give one pause.

THE GIRL

Well, at least we begin with futility. Most marriages take years to arrive there.

ARTHUR

Don't be saucy, Evelyn.

THE GIRL

(*Earnestly*)

Oh, Arthur, I wouldn't suggest marriage if I thought it was utterly unfeasible. I think we can make a go of it. I really do. I know you have no faith in my exorcism . . .

ARTHUR

As I say, it may be an effective shock therapy.

THE GIRL

But we could get married this minute, and I still think we

could make a go of it. I'm not a dangerous schizophrenic; I just hallucinate. I could keep your house for you. I did for my father very competently before he remarried. I'm a good cook, and you do find me attractive, don't you? I love you, Arthur. You are really very good for me. I retain reality remarkably well with you. I know I could be a good wife. Many schizophrenics function quite well if one has faith in them.

ARTHUR

(*Touched by her earnestness*)
My dear Evelyn . . .

THE GIRL

I don't ask you to have faith in dybbuks or gods or exorcisms—just in me.
(*He gently touches her cheek.*)

ARTHUR

How in heaven's name did we reach this point of talking marriage?

THE GIRL

It is a common point of discussion between people in love.
(*He kneels before her, takes her hand between his.*)

ARTHUR

(*Tenderly*)
I do not love you. Nor do you love me. We met five hours ago and exchanged the elementary courtesy of conversation—the rest is your own ingenuousness.

THE GIRL

I do not remember ever being as happy as I am this moment. I feel enchanted. (*They are terribly close now. He leans to her, his*

127

arm moving to embrace her. And then he stops, and the moment is broken. He turns away, scowls, stands) You are in full flight again, aren't you?

ARTHUR

I reserve a certain low level of morality which includes not taking advantage of incompetent minors.

THE GIRL

Why can't you believe that I love you?

ARTHUR

(*Angrily*)
I simply do not believe anybody loves anyone. Let's have an end to this. (*He is abruptly aware that their entire love scene has been observed by the old men, who are clustered together in the open doorway of* THE RABBI's *office, beaming at them. With a furious sigh,* ARTHUR *strides to the door and shuts it in the old men's faces. He turns back to* THE GIRL, *scowling*) Really, this is all much too fanciful. Really, it is. In an hour, you will be back to your institution, where I may or may not visit you.
(THE GIRL *sits down slowly*.)

THE GIRL

If I were not already insane, the thought that I might not see you again would make me so.

ARTHUR

I don't know what you want of me.

THE GIRL

(*One step from tears*)
I want you to find the meaning of your life in me.

128

ARTHUR

But that's insane. How can you ask such an impossible thing?

THE GIRL

Because you love me.

ARTHUR

(*Cries out*)

I don't know what you mean by love! All it means to me is I shall buy you a dinner, take you to the theatre, and then straight to our tryst, where I shall reach under your blouse for the sake of tradition while you breathe hotly in my ear in a pretense of passion. We will mutter automatic endearments, nibbling at the sweat on each other's earlobes, all the while gracelessly fumbling with buttons and zippers, cursing under our breath the knots in our shoelaces, and telling ourselves that this whole comical business of stripping off our trousers is an act of nature like the pollination of weeds. Even in that one brief moment when our senses finally obliterate our individual alonenesses, we will hear ringing in our ears the reluctant creaking of mattress springs.

(THE GIRL *stares at him, awed by this bitter expostulation.*)

THE GIRL

You are possessed.

ARTHUR

At your age, I suppose, one still finds theatrical charm in this ultimate of fantasies, but when you have been backstage as often as I have, you will discover love to be an altogether shabby business of cold creams and costumes.

THE GIRL

(*Staring at him*)

You are possessed by a dybbuk that does not allow you to love.

ARTHUR

(*Crying out again in sudden anguish*)

Oh, leave me alone! Let's get on with this wretched exorcism!
(*He strides to the door, suddenly turns, confused, disturbed, and would say something, but he doesn't know what. He opens the door to find the old men patiently waiting for him with beaming smiles. This disconcerts him and he turns to* THE GIRL *again and is again at a loss for words. She stares at the floor.*)

THE GIRL

We could be very happy if you would have faith in me.
(*He turns and shuffles out of* THE RABBI's *office.*)

ARTHUR

(*To the old men*)

It was tasteless of you to gawk at us.
(*He continues into the synagogue, trailed by the old men. He sits, and is immediately surrounded by the old men.*)

FOREMAN

Are you interested in this girl, young man, because my son is not a rich man, by any means, but he will give you a fine wedding, catered by good people, with a cantor . . .

ZITORSKY

And a choir.

FOREMAN

. . . Possibly, and a dowry perhaps in the amount of five hundred dollars which, believe me, is more than he can afford. However, I am told you are a professional man, a lawyer, and the father of the bride must lay out good money for such a catch.

ALPER *and* ZITORSKY

Sure . . . Absolutely.

FOREMAN

Of course, the girl is an incompetent and you will have to apply
to the courts to be appointed the committee of her person . . .

ALPER

. . . A formality, I assure you, once you have married her.

FOREMAN

As for the girl, I can tell you first hand, she is a fine Jewish
girl . . .

ZITORSKY

Modest . . .

ALPER

Devout . . .

FOREMAN

. . . And she bakes first-rate pastries.

ARTHUR

(*Staring at the gay old men with disbelief*)

You are all mad, madder than the girl, and if I don't get out of
here soon, I shall be as mad as the rest.

ZITORSKY

A beauty, young man. Listen, it is said—better a full-bosomed
wife than to marry a Rothschild.

SCHLISSEL

Leave the man alone. We have all been miserably married for

half a century ourselves. How can you in good faith recommend the institution?

ALPER

The girl is so obviously taken with him. It would be a good match.

FOREMAN
(*Anxiously*)
Perhaps, he is married already.

ALPER
(*To* ARTHUR)
My dear fellow, how wonderful to be in love.

ARTHUR

I love nothing!

THE CABALIST

Yes. The girl is quite right. He is possessed. He loves nothing. Love is an act of faith, and yours is a faithless generation. That is your dybbuk.
(*The front door of the synagogue opens, and* THE SEXTON *slips quickly in, quietly closing the door.*)

ARTHUR
(*To* THE CABALIST)
Don't you think it's time to get on with this exorcism?

THE CABALIST

Yes.
(*He moves to the door of* THE RABBI's *office, where he regards the supine form of* THE GIRL *on the couch.*)

ALPER

(*To* THE SEXTON)

Did you get anybody?

(THE SEXTON *moves in his nervous way down into the synagogue. He has obviously been on the go since he left; sweat beads his brow, and he is breathing heavily.*)

THE SEXTON

(*Unbuttoning his coat and wiping his brow*)

Gentlemen, we are in the soup.

SCHLISSEL

You couldn't find anybody?

THE SEXTON

Actually, we have nine now, but the issue of a quorum has become an academic one. Oh, let me catch my breath. The Rabbi will be here in a few minutes.

ALPER

The Rabbi?

THE SEXTON

I saw him on Woodhaven Boulevard, and he said he would join us. Harris is on his way already. I saw him coming down the hill from his house. But the whole matter is academic.

ALPER

You told the Rabbi we need him to exorcise the girl's dybbuk?

THE SEXTON

Well, what else was I to say? He asked me what I needed a quorum for at one o'clock in the afternoon, and I told him, and he thought for a moment, and he said: "All right, I'll be there in

133

a few minutes." He is quite a nice fellow, something of a press agent perhaps, but with good intentions. Oh, I am perspiring like an animal. I shall surely have the ague tomorrow. I have been running all over looking for Jews. I even went to Friedman the tailor. He wasn't even in town. So let me tell you. I was running back here. I turned the corner on Thirty-Third Road there, and I see parked right in front of the synagogue a police patrol car.

(*The others start.*)

ALPER

(*Looking up*)

Oh?

THE SEXTON

That's what I mean when I say we are in the soup.

SCHLISSEL

Did they say something to you?

THE SEXTON

Sure they said something. I tell you, my heart gave such a turn when I saw that police car there. They were sitting there, those two policemen, big strapping cossacks with dark faces like avenging angels, smoking cigarettes, and with their revolvers bulging through their blue overcoats. As I walked across the street to the synagogue, my knees were knocking.

ALPER

When was this? It was just now?

THE SEXTON

Just this second. Just before I came in the door . . . Hello, Harris, how are you?

(*This last to the octogenarian, who, bundled in his heavy*

134

*overcoat, muffler, and with his hat pulled down on his
head, has just entered the synagogue.*)

ZITORSKY

(*To* THE SEXTON)

So what happened?

HARRIS

(*In his high shrill voice, as he unbuttons his overcoat*)
Gentlemen! Have you heard about this dybbuk?

SCHLISSEL

Harris, we were all here at the time he called you.

THE SEXTON

Harris, did you see the police car outside?

SCHLISSEL

So what did the policeman say?

THE SEXTON

(*Unbuttoning his collar and wiping his neck with a handker-
chief*)
This big strapping fellow with his uniform full of buttons
looks up, he says: "You know a man named David Foreman?
We're looking for him and his granddaughter, a girl, eighteen
years old." Well?! Eh! Well, are we in the soup or not?
    (SCHLISSEL *goes to the front door, opens it a conspiratorial
crack, and looks out.*)

ARTHUR

I don't think the police will bother you if you get your exorcism started right away. They won't interrupt a religious ceremony, especially if they don't know what it is.

THE CABALIST

(*Who has made up his own mind*)
Sexton, fetch the black candles, one for each man.
(THE SEXTON *scurries to* THE RABBI's *office, where the black candles are lying on the desk, wrapped in brown grocery paper.*)

ARTHUR

(*Moving to the front door*)
I'll stand by the door and talk to the police if they come in.

SCHLISSEL

(*Closing the front door*)
They're out there all right.

THE CABALIST

(*He looks about the little synagogue, immensely dignified now, almost beatified in his authority. The others wait on his words*)
I shall want to perform the ablutions of the Cohanim. Is there a Levite among you?

SCHLISSEL

I am a Levite.

THE CABALIST

You shall pour the water on my hands.
(THE SEXTON *scoots across the synagogue, carrying black candles to everyone.*)

HARRIS

(*Looking distractedly about*)
What are we doing now? Where is the dybbuk?

ALPER

Harris, put on a prayer shawl.

HARRIS

(*Moving nervously to the office door*)
Is this actually a serious business then? Where is the dybbuk?
Tell me because Bleyer the Sexton told me nothing . . .
  (*His words drift off into a mumble. He enters the office,
  sees* THE GIRL *sitting rigidly on the chair. He starts at the
  sight of her, snatches a prayer shawl from the carton, and,
  quite in terror, darts back into the synagogue.*)

THE CABALIST

There is nothing in the Book of Codes which gives the pro-
cedure for exorcism, so I have selected those passages to read that
I thought most apt. For the purpose of cleansing our souls, we
shall recite the Al-chait, and we shall recite that prayer of atonement which begins: "Sons of man such as sit in darkness." As
you pray these prayers, let the image of God in any of His
seventy-two faces rise before you.

ALPER

(*Crossing into* THE RABBI'S *office*)
I'll get the books.

THE SEXTON

(*Giving* SCHLISSEL *a metal bowl and a pitcher*)
Fill it with water.

SCHLISSEL

I'm an atheist. Why am I mixed up in all this?

ALPER

We do not have a quorum. Will this be valid?

137

THE CABALIST

We will let God decide.

THE SEXTON

When shall I blow the ram's horn?

THE CABALIST

I shall instruct you when.

HARRIS

(*Putting on his shawl*)

What shall I do? Where shall I stand?

ZITORSKY

(*To* HARRIS)

Stand here, and do not be afraid.

(FOREMAN *comes out of* THE RABBI's *office carrying a long white woolen prayer shawl, which he gives to* ARTHUR.)

FOREMAN

(*To* ARTHUR)

I will show you how to put it on.

(*He helps* ARTHUR *enshroud himself in the prayer shawl.* SCHLISSEL *comes out of the washroom carefully carrying his brass bowl and the pitcher filled with water. He goes to* THE CABALIST, *who holds his white hands over the basin.* SCHLISSEL *carefully pours the water over them.* THE CABALIST *speaks with great distinctness.*)

THE CABALIST

"Blessed art Thou, O Lord our God, King of the Universe, who hath sanctified us by his commandments, and has commanded us to cleanse our hands."

ALL

Amen.

(*The others watch until the last of the water has been poured over his hands. A sudden silence settles over the synagogue. They are all standing about now, eight men, cloaked in white, holding their prayer books.* THE CABALIST *dries his hands on a towel handed to him by* SCHLISSEL. *He puts the towel down, rolls his sleeves down, takes his long shawl and, with a sweep of his arms, raises it over his head, lifts his face, and cries out—*)

THE CABALIST

"Thou knowest the secrets of eternity and the most hidden mysteries of all living. Thou searchest the innermost recesses, and tryest the reins and the heart. Nought is concealed from thee, or hidden from thine eyes. May it then be thy will, O Lord our God and God of our fathers, to forgive us for all our sins, to pardon us for all our iniquities, and to grant us remission for all our transgressions."

(*As one, the other old men sweep their shawls over their heads and begin the ancient recital of their sins. They all face the Ark, standing in their places, bending and twisting at the knees and beating upon their breasts with the clenched fists of their right hands. They all pray individually, lifting their voices in a wailing of the spirit.* ARTHUR *remains silent.*)

ALL

"For the sin which we have committed before thee under compulsion, or of our own will;

And for the sin which we have committed before thee in hardening of the heart!

For the sin which we have committed before thee unknow-
ingly:"

ZITORSKY

"And for the sin which we have committed before thee with ut-
terance of the lips."

FOREMAN

"For the sin which we have committed before thee by un-
chastity;"

SCHLISSEL

"For the sin which we have committed before thee by scoffing;"

HARRIS

"For the sin which we have committed before thee by slander;
And for the sin which we have committed before thee by the
stretched-forth neck of pride:"
> (*It is a deadly serious business, this gaunt confessional.
> The spectacle of the eight men, cloaked in white, crying
> out into the air the long series of their sins and their pleas
> for remission, has a suggestion of the fearsome barbarism
> of the early Hebrews. They stand, eyes closed, and in the
> fervor of communication with God, their faces pained
> with penitence. The last of the old men, HARRIS, finally
> cries out the last lines of supplication, his thin voice all
> alone in the hush of the synagogue*)

"And also for the sins for which we are liable to any of the four
death penalties inflicted by the court—stoning, burning, be-
heading, and strangling; for thou art the forgiver of Israel
and the pardoner of the tribes of Jeshurun in every genera-

tion and beside thee we have no king, who pardoneth and forgiveth."

(*Again, the silence falls over the stage.*)

THE CABALIST

"Children of men, such as sit in darkness and in the shadow of death, being bound in affliction and iron, He brought them out of darkness, and the shadow of death."

THE OTHERS

"Children of men, such as sit in darkness and in the shadow of death, being bound in affliction and iron, He brought them out of darkness, and the shadow of death."

THE CABALIST

"Fools because of their transgressions, and because of their iniquities are afflicted."

THE OTHERS

"Fools because of their transgressions and because of their iniquities are afflicted."

THE CABALIST

"They cry unto The Lord in their trouble, and He saveth them out of their distress."

(*The repetition of the lines has its cumulative effect on* ARTHUR. *His lips begin to move involuntarily, and soon he has joined the others, quietly muttering the words.*)

ARTHUR *and* THE OTHERS

"They cry unto The Lord in their trouble, and He saveth them out of their distress."

THE CABALIST

"Then He is gracious unto him and saith:"

ARTHUR *and* THE OTHERS

"Then He is gracious unto him and saith:"

THE CABALIST

"Deliver him from going down to the pit; I have found a ransom."

ARTHUR *and* THE OTHERS

"Deliver him from going down to the pit; I have found a ransom."

THE CABALIST

Amen.

ARTHUR *and* THE OTHERS

Amen.

THE CABALIST

Bring the girl in, Mr. Foreman.
(FOREMAN *nods and goes into* THE RABBI's *office.*)

ALPER

(*To* SCHLISSEL)

I don't like it. Even if the Rabbi comes, there will only be nine of us. I am a traditionalist. Without a quorum of ten, it won't work.

SCHLISSEL

(*Muttering*)

So what do you want me to do?
(*In* THE RABBI's *office,* FOREMAN *touches* THE GIRL's *shoul-*

*der, and she starts from her comalike state and looks
at him.)*

FOREMAN

Come. It is time.

*(She nods nervously and sits up. There is a vacuous look
about her, the vague, distracted look of the insane.)*

THE GIRL

(Quite numbly)

Where are you taking me? My mother is in Rome. They put
the torch to her seven sons, and they hold her hostage. *(She
rises in obedience to her grandfather's arm as he gently escorts
her out of the office into the synagogue proper. All the while she
maintains a steady drone of rattling gibberish)* Where were
you yesterday? I asked everybody about you. You should have
been here. We had a lot of fun. We had a party, and there were
thousands of people, Calebites and Bedouins, dancing like
gypsies.

*(She suddenly lapses into a sullen silence, staring at the
ground, her shoulders jerking involuntarily. The others
regard her uneasily.)*

THE SEXTON

Shall I take the ram's horn out?

THE CABALIST

Yes.

*(THE SEXTON produces the horn-shaped trumpet from the
base of the pulpit. The front door of the synagogue now
opens, and a tall, strapping young POLICEMAN, heavy with
the authority of his thick blue overcoat, steps one step
into the synagogue. He stands in the open doorway, one*

143

hand on the latch of the door, his attitude quite brusque—
as if he could not possibly get his work done if he had to
be polite.)

THE POLICEMAN

Is Rabbi Marks here?
(ALPER *throws up his arms in despair. The others alter-*
nately stare woodenly at THE POLICEMAN *or down at the*
floor. ARTHUR, *still deeply disturbed, rubs his brow.* THE
CABALIST *begins to pray silently, only his lips moving in*
rapid supplication.)

THE SEXTON

No, he's not.

THE POLICEMAN

I'm looking for a girl named Evelyn Foreman. Is that the girl?
(*He indicates* THE GIRL.)

ALPER

(*Moving away, muttering*)
Is there any need, Officer, to be so brusque or to stand in an
open doorway so that we all chill to our bones?

THE POLICEMAN

(*Closing the door behind him*)
Sorry.

SCHLISSEL

(*To* ZITORSKY)
A real cossack, eh? What a brute. He will take us all to the
station house and beat us with night sticks.

THE POLICEMAN

(*A little more courteously*)

A girl named Evelyn Foreman. Her father has put out a call for her. She's missing from her home. He said she might be here with her grandfather. Is there a Mr. David Foreman here?

(*Nobody says anything.*)

ALPER

You are interrupting a service, Officer.

THE POLICEMAN

I'm sorry. Just tell me, is that the girl? I'll call in and tell them we found her.

(SCHLISSEL *suddenly advances on* THE POLICEMAN.)

SCHLISSEL

First of all, where do you come to walk in here like you were raiding a poolroom? This is a synagogue, you animal. Have a little respect.

THE POLICEMAN

All right, all right, I'm sorry. I happen to be Jewish myself.

(ALPER *looks up quickly.*)

ALPER

You're Jewish? (ALPER *turns slowly to* THE SEXTON) Sexton, our tenth man.

THE SEXTON

Alper, are you crazy?

ALPER

A fine, strapping Jewish boy. (*To* THE POLICEMAN) Listen, we need a tenth. You'll help us out, won't you?

145

SCHLISSEL

(*Strolling nervously past* ALPER)
Alper, what are you doing, for God's sakes?

ALPER

We have to have ten men.

SCHLISSEL

What kind of prank is this? You are an impossible rogue, do you know that?

ALPER

(*Taking* SCHLISSEL *aside*)
What are you getting so excited about? He doesn't have to know what it is. We'll tell him it's a wedding. I think it's funny.

SCHLISSEL

Well, we will see how funny it is when they take us to the basement of the police station and beat us with their night sticks.

ALPER

Night sticks. Really, Schlissel, you are a romantic. (*Advancing on* THE POLICEMAN) I tell you, Officer, it would really help us out if you would stay ten or fifteen minutes. This girl—if you really want to know—is about to be married, and what is going on here is the Ritual of Shriving.

ZITORSKY

Shriving?

ALPER

A sort of ceremony of purification. It is a ritual not too commonly practiced any more, and I suggest you will find it quite interesting.

146

HARRIS
(*To* SCHLISSEL)
What is he talking about?

SCHLISSEL
Who knows?
(THE POLICEMAN *opens the door and calls to his colleague outside.*)

THE POLICEMAN
I'll be out in about ten minutes, Tommy, all right? (*He opens the door wider for* THE RABBI, *who now comes hurrying into the synagogue, still carrying his briefcase*) Hello, Rabbi, how are you?
(THE RABBI *frowns, a little confused at* THE POLICEMAN'S *presence.*)

THE RABBI
Hello, Officer, what are you doing here?
(*He moves quickly to his office, taking stock of everything as he goes: the seven old men and* ARTHUR *in their white shawls, and* THE GIRL *standing woodenly in the center of the synagogue.* ALPER *and* ZITORSKY *greet him with hellos, at which he nods back.*)

THE POLICEMAN
They've asked me to make a tenth for the shriving.

THE RABBI
(*Frowning as he darts into his office*)
Shriving? (*He opens his desk to get out his own large white shawl, unbuttoning his coat as he does. He notes* ALPER, *who has*

Rabbi enters

147

followed him to the doorway) What is the policeman doing here?

ALPER

We needed a tenth.

(*In the synagogue,* THE POLICEMAN *speaks amiably to* ZITORSKY.)

THE POLICEMAN

This is the girl, isn't it? (ZITORSKY *nods his head bleakly*) What's really going on here?

(*In* THE RABBI'S *office,* THE RABBI *sweeps his large shawl over his shoulders.*)

ALPER

We have said Al-chait and a prayer of atonement, and we are waiting now just for you.

(THE RABBI *frowns in troubled thought, slips his skullcap on as he slips his fedora off. In the synagogue,* ZITORSKY *shuffles to* SCHLISSEL.)

ZITORSKY

(*Indicating* THE POLICEMAN *with his head, he mutters*) He knows, he knows.

SCHLISSEL

Of course. Did Alper expect to get away with such a collegiate prank?

(*In* THE RABBI'S *office,* THE RABBI *finishes a rapid, silent prayer, standing with his eyes closed. He looks up at* ALPER *now.*)

THE RABBI

I would rather not take any active role in this exorcism. I am not quite sure of my rabbinical position. But it would please me a great deal to believe once again in a God of dybbuks. (*He walks quickly past* ALPER *out into the synagogue.* ALPER *follows*) Well, we are ten.

(*A silence falls upon the gathered men.*)

FOREMAN

May God look upon us with the eye of mercy and understanding and may He forgive us if we sin in our earnestness.

THE OTHERS

Amen.

THE CABALIST

Sexton, light the candles. (THE SEXTON *lights each man's candle.* THE CABALIST *advances slowly to* THE GIRL, *who stands slackly, her body making small occasional jerking movements, apparently in a schizophrenic state.* THE CABALIST *slowly draws a line before* THE GIRL *with the flat of his toe. He speaks quietly*) Dybbuk, I draw this line beyond which you may not come. You may not do harm to anyone in this room. (*The old men shift nervously in their various positions around the synagogue.* THE CABALIST *turns to* THE SEXTON) Open the Ark. (THE SEXTON *moves quickly up to the altar and opens the brown sliding doors of the Ark, exposing the several scrolls within, standing in their handsome velvet coverings.* THE CABALIST *moves slowly back to his original position; he says quietly—*) Dybbuk, you are in the presence of God and His Holy Scrolls. (THE GIRL *gasps*) I plead with you one last time to leave the body of this girl. (*There is no answer*) Then I will invoke the curse of excommunication upon your pitiable soul. Sexton, blow Tekiah. (THE SEXTON *raises the ram's horn to his lips, and the eerie, frightening tones shrill out into the hushed air*) Sexton, blow Shevurim. (*Again,*

149

THE SEXTON *raises the ram's horn and blows a variation of the first hollow tones*) Sexton, blow Teruah. (*A third time,* THE SEXTON *blows a variation of the original tones*) Sexton, blow the Great Tekiah, and, upon the sound of these tones, dybbuk, you will be wrenched from the girl's body and there will be cast upon you the final anathema of excommunication from all the world of the living and from all the world of the dead. Sexton, blow the Great Tekiah.

> (*For the fourth time,* THE SEXTON *raises the ram's horn to his lips and blows a quick succession of loud blasts. A silence falls heavily on the gathered men, the notes fading into the air. Nothing happens.* THE GIRL *remains as she was, standing slackly, her hands making involuntary little movements.* FOREMAN's *head sinks slowly on his chest, and an expression of deep pain covers his face.* THE CABALIST *stares steadily at* THE GIRL. *Suddenly,* ARTHUR *begins to moan softly, and then with swift violence a horrible scream tears out of his throat. He staggers one brief step forward. At the peak of his scream, he falls heavily down on the floor of the synagogue in a complete faint. The echoes of his scream tingle momentarily in the high corners of the air in the synagogue. The others stand petrified for a moment, staring at his slack body on the floor.*)

ALPER

My God. I think what has happened is that we have exorcised the wrong dybbuk.

> (THE POLICEMAN *starts toward* ARTHUR's *limp body.*)

THE POLICEMAN

All right, don't crowd around. Let him breathe.

150

THE CABALIST

He will be all right in a moment.

ZITORSKY

If I didn't see this with my own eyes, I wouldn't believe it.

THE RABBI

Mr. Hirschman, will he be all right?

THE CABALIST

Yes.

SCHLISSEL

(*With simple devoutness*)

Praise be to the Lord, for His compassion is everywhere.

(HARRIS *sinks down onto a chair, exhausted and terrified by the whole experience.* THE RABBI *moves slowly down and stares at* ARTHUR *as* SCHLISSEL, ZITORSKY *and* ALPER *help him to a chair.*)

ALPER

How are you, my dear fellow?

ARTHUR

(*Still in a state of shock*)

I don't know.

THE SEXTON

(*Coming forward with some wine*)

Would you like a sip of wine?

ARTHUR

(*Taking the goblet*)

Yes, thank you very much. (*Turning to look at* THE GIRL)
How is she?

(*Her schizophrenic state is quite obvious.* ARTHUR *turns
back, his face furrowed and his eyes closed now in a mask
of pain.*)

SCHLISSEL

Was it a painful experience, my friend?

ARTHUR

I don't know. I feel beyond pain. (*Indeed, his hands are visibly
trembling as if from cold; his face is rigid and masklike. Words
become more difficult to say*) I feel as if I have been reduced to
the moment of birth, as if the universe has become one hunger.
(*He seems to be almost on the verge of collapse.*)

ALPER

A hunger for what?

ARTHUR

(*Whispering*)

I don't know.

THE CABALIST

For life.

(*At these words,* ARTHUR *sinks back into his chair, exhausted.*)

ARTHUR

Yes, for life. I want to live. (*He opens his eyes and begins to
pray quietly*) God of my fathers, you have exorcised all truth
as I knew it out of me. You have taken away my reason and

definition. Give me then a desire to wake in the morning, a passion for the things of life, a pleasure in work, a purpose to sorrow . . . (*He slowly stands, for a reason unknown even to himself, and turns to regard the slouched figure of* THE GIRL) Give me all of these things in one—give me the ability to love. (*In a hush of the scene, he moves slowly to* THE GIRL *and stands before her crouched slack figure*) Dybbuk, hear me. I will cherish this girl, and give her a home. I will tend to her needs and hold her in my arms when she screams out with your voice. Her soul is mine now—her soul, her charm, her beauty—even you, her insanity, are mine. If God will not exorcise you, dybbuk, I will. (*To* THE GIRL) Evelyn, I will get your coat. We have a lot of things to do this afternoon. (*He turns to the others*) It is not a simple matter to get somebody released from an institution in New York. (*He starts briskly across to* THE RABBI's *office and pauses at the door*) Officer, why don't you just call in and say you have located the girl and she is being brought to her father. (*To* MR. FOREMAN) You'd better come along with us. Would somebody get my coat? We will need her father's approval. We shall have to stop off at my office and have my secretary draw some papers.

> (MR. FOREMAN *has hurriedly gotten* THE GIRL's *coat,* ARTHUR's *coat, and his own. In this rather enchanted state, these three drift to the exit door.*)

THE POLICEMAN

Rabbi, is this all right?

THE RABBI

Yes, quite all right.

ARTHUR

(*Pausing at the door, bemused, enchanted*)

Oh—thank you all. Good-bye.

ALL

Good-bye.

ZITORSKY

Go in good health.

ALPER

Come back and make a tenth for us sometime.

(ARTHUR *smiles and herds* THE GIRL *and* FOREMAN *out of the synagogue. The door closes behind them.*)

SCHLISSEL

(*Sitting with a deep sigh*)

Well, what is one to say? An hour ago, he didn't believe in God; now he's exorcising dybbuks.

ALPER

(*Pulling up a chair*)

He still doesn't believe in God. He simply wants to love. (ZITORSKY *joins the other two*) And when you stop and think about it, gentlemen, is there any difference? Let us make a supposition . . .

(*As the curtain falls, life as it was slowly returns to the synagogue. The three old men engage in disputation,* THE CABALIST *returns to his isolated studies,* THE RABBI *moves off into his office,* THE SEXTON *finds a chore for himself, and* THE POLICEMAN *begins to button his coat.*)

The Curtain Falls

ABOUT THE AUTHOR

PADDY CHAYEFSKY was born in New York City in 1923. He graduated from De Witt Clinton High School and C.C.N.Y. before enlisting in the Army during World War II. In Germany he ran afoul of a booby trap that put him in the hospital where, while convalescing, he wrote the book and lyrics for the army musical, *No T.O. for Love.* He thus came to the attention of Garson Kanin, who invited him to help in the writing of the award-winning documentary, *True Glory.* After the war he worked briefly in his uncle's print shop, then turned to writing for movies, radio and television. He rose rapidly to prominence with such television scripts as *Marty, Bachelor Party, Middle of the Night, The Mother, The Big Deal* and *The Catered Affair. Marty,* which won the Academy Award, was the first television play to be successfully made into a motion picture. The film version of *Bachelor Party* was a United States entry at the Cannes Film Festival. Chayefsky's first original screenplay, *The Goddess,* won the Critics Prize at the 1958 Brussels Film Festival. His first play for Broadway, *Middle of the Night,* ran for almost two years, was then produced as a motion picture by Chayefsky's own company and was chosen as the official American film for the Cannes Film Festival.